Anonymous

Communications from the Spirit World given by Lorenzo Dow

Anonymous

Communications from the Spirit World given by Lorenzo Dow

ISBN/EAN: 9783337216474

Printed in Europe, USA, Canada, Australia, Japan

Cover: Foto ©Lupo / pixelio.de

More available books at **www.hansebooks.com**

COMMUNICATIONS

FROM

THE SPIRIT WORLD,

GIVEN BY

LORENZO DOW,

AND OTHERS.

———

THROUGH A LADY.

══════

NEW YORK:

PRINTED BY A. J. BRADY, 5 TRYON ROW.

1861.

CONTENTS.

INTRODUCTION.

THE object of the following Communications, my friends, is to give you in the simplest and most practical form, the main teachings of Spiritualism.

We have not entered into discussion or argument ; but we have put plainly before you, your duties as followers of those high and holy influences that are now coming so directly in *rapport* with your earth, and who will take up their abode in the hearts of every one of you, if you will only so live as to draw them to you. They are waiting patiently at the doors of *your* hearts. Will ye not open unto them? Will ye not be partakers of the blessed baptism of the true spirit, and enjoy, while yet on Earth, a foretaste of Heaven?

We leave our little book to take care of itself, trusting that the truths it teaches may come home to many, and give them a higher and more correct sense of their

4

duties, as Spiritualists, than they have heretofore had; showing, as it does, the necessity for each man to commence the work of reformation in himself, before he attempts to correct or reform others; and the absolute necessity there is for him to follow out the teaching of the olden time, so long laid aside, namely: "To do to every man, as he would have every man do to him."

LORENZO DOW.

ON THE MEDIUMS.

THE mediums, as a class, are lamentably deficient in a true knowledge of their high and holy office. Seeming to think physical manifestations the only ones worth seeking, they entirely lose sight of the beautiful mystery hidden (yet not unattainable) in the higher teachings of Spiritualism—the total change it can produce in our moral characters ; the universal love of all mankind, as fellow-travellers and co-workers in this earth life ; the desire to aid and forward each in their individual aims after happiness ; elevating and encouraging the weak and sinful ; raising the lowly and oppressed, and in every conceivable way endeavoring to do good. Such should be the teachings and actions of media. I myself, an itinerant preacher while on the earth, know from experience what good can be accomplished in this way ; and now, with my more extended vision, I am more and more deeply impressed that this is the highest benefit that media should aim to effect.

"Is not he that subdueth himself greater than he that taketh a city?" Thorough self-control, and self-abnegation, must be the first aim of a medium intending to be useful in the manner I have stated. Selfishness, self-indulgence, false pride, all that militates against this universal love, must be done away with, and a desire to benefit the whole human family be the governing principle. When this wholesome state of feeling shall attain footing, and really work among men, what a change will be seen ! Vice and crime will gradually die out, and a true millenium of happiness and peace be established.

Mediums may, perhaps, think, from what I have said,

that I disapprove of the physical manifestations alto-gether. But it is not so. They have all been neces-sary so far, and in some cases are so still. But, for *convinced* Spiritualists and media to have no higher de-sires than to hear raps, tips, and so forth, and little communications from their departed relatives, testifying that they are near, I disapprove altogether. When once the fact of the truth of spirit intercourse is con-firmed to you, then I want you to press on, and find out the motives of spirits in coming; and you (if seek-ing truly) will soon see that there is more in this than the mere gratification of your curiosity, or even of your affections.

Spirits have a work to do here, and they want you to help them, as it is only through men they can work effi-ciently. By impressions on hearts open to receive them, they can do much; but they would be able to do far more, could they find media, not only to speak these necessary truths through, but who were so imbued with the spirit of them, that their daily life should be a living out of the spirits' teachings through them. Some few there are of this stamp, but sadly too few for the immense field there is to labor in; and we write these words now, in the hope of awakening some others, who are more indifferent than wicked, to see the importance of the mission given to them, and that they may be led to feel the necessity of making all conformable—lives and teachings—teachings and lives—if they desire to do good in their generation. Woe, to the unfaithful mediums who, having the gift of Holy Spirit, abuse it to their own purposes. Woe, to those who, lusting after wealth and the gauds of earth-life, traffic with the gift God has given them to enlighten and benefit their fellow-mortals. What unhappiness is theirs here! What condemnation shall be hereafter! How would they tremble, and quake, and wish they might never

have had this glorious gift, could they for a moment
see the anguish they are laying up for themselves, by
their unfaithful stewardship! Repent, ye mediums! or
your lamps will be taken from you, and ye be thrust into
outer darkness. While ye possess the godlike gift, try
to reform yourselves. Cast out the evil from your own
hearts, and evil spirits will no longer stay near you ;
they have not the power to injure, if you are only true
to yourselves. As like attracts like, so they haunt
you and help you in your wickedness. But they could
not do so if you were true and faithful to yourselves.
They would gladly rise through you, if you only took
the right measures to assist them. When they come, it
is for that purpose ; but, by *your* sinning, you only
plunge *them* into deeper darkness ; for, instead of encouraging them to do better, you foster their former
vices, and make them have a stronger hold. Unhappy
spirits, who come to such mediums! Unhappy mediums, to draw such spirits to them ! -

My dear media, and Spiritualist friends, I would say
a few words more to you before I leave, to encourage
you in your work. You cannot see what a great and
glorious work you are engaged in, but you can, many
of you in yourselves, realize the happiness and peace
spirit intercourse of the right kind can bestow. Many
of you who have not yet found this out, will, I trust,
soon do so ; and, as your aims after it are more and
more elevated, so more and more shall be given to you,
and you, in your turn, shall be the means of conveying
it to others. You will be so happy yourselves, you will
not be contented unless you make others around you
feel the same, and the desire will bring its own fulfil-
ment. This is the great aim of Spiritualism ; to make
mankind happy. Happy in the true sense. Happy, and
consequently good. A man at peace with himself,
would not feel disposed to quarrel with his neighbor.

That this universal harmony may the sooner be attained, mediums especially are called upon to teach as I have said, and to practice what they teach.

L. D.

September 19th, 1860.

ON INFLUENCE.

THE beautiful influence that good spirits strive to exercise over mortals, bringing them into harmony with themselves and with nature—this shall be the subject of our theme this morning; and we will endeavor to make clear to all the importance of it, and the vital interests that are at stake in its right appreciation.

The unseen world is filled with spirits of different kinds, some highly developed, others comparatively low and debased, but all striving to gain a foothold in the hearts of the human family—the former to benefit mankind, the latter themselves. Where there are aspirations and desires for a holier and purer life, these holy and pure spirits find a lodging. They can enter in and dwell there, and by their influence produce the desired results, and with them a peace and joy, a trusting and comforting reliance on their aid, that can remove all anxiety, fear, or doubt, under the most trying circumstances. Joyous and glad, the truly spiritualized man wends on his way; trials may beset him, but his faith, strong in the promises, and buoyed up by the Heavenly magnetism of his spirit guides, never fails; he knows they are around to help him, and, if they cannot avert misfortunes, they can make them so light to him, and sometimes so useful to his further development, that they may rather be considered blessings.

I would not, by this, infer that man must trust all to the spirits, and neglect to help himself. Far otherwise. Man must be his own provider. Spirits can assist, but they cannot supersede a man or woman in their own duties; and woful would be the state of families left

with no other resources than their trust in spirit help
for mundane assistance. The design of the spirits is
not to do what we came into the world to do for our-
selves, but to make us happy and harmonious while
doing it—to influence us to do right, to avoid evil, to
conquer all wrong feelings, to subdue all evil tempers,
to feel love and kindness for all, irrespective of station,
education or morals ; in fact, to follow in the footsteps
of that blessed Teacher who has so long waited in
patient expectation that the world might follow His
teachings, and who is still ready to give His influence
to help them to do so.

As I said at the beginning, there are two kinds of
influences always at work. If the one is neglected, the
other steps in, and, in place of producing harmony and
peace, discords and divisions ensue. The evils to be
apprehended from these latter cannot be estimated.
Gently and insiduously they approach ; finding something in the mind they wish to influence similar to
themselves, they work upon and cultivate that passion,
taste or feeling, and, after obtaining a lodgment in one
little corner, soon control the whole—magnetize the
man or woman to see with their eyes, hear with their
ears, and understand as they wish them. Wonderful
is the control they can obtain over a mortal if he yields
himself up willingly a slave to them. Revenge may
appear a virtue ; murder, retributive justice ; unjust
anger, just censure; pride, an ennobling virtue ; un-
charitable remarks, necessary to show our contempt of
such and such failings—never looking within on the
dark foul mass of passions engendered in their own
bosoms. Such influences as these never lead to self-
examination—self-knowledge. To hide the true character from themselves is the aim of these dangerous
inmates. Believing themselves perfect, or rather trying
to believe themselves right, men stumble on into deeper

spirit darkness. Sometimes good influences may prevail and enlighten the poor deluded ones, but hard is the struggle to penetrate, and very difficult to dislodge the former tenants of the soul. Far easier to prevent, by timely care, their first entrance ; then they are weak, and easily expelled, but strength is daily added by their being permitted to remain.

Some may say, How can any one be safe? If such influences are here always ready to step in, who can be secure? Only they, my friends, who, in earnest simplicity and confiding trust, pray and strive while they pray, for those holy influences that can and will protect and defend them against all others. By praying, I do not mean repeating long formulas, on their knees, till mind and body are fatigued and inharmonious, but the constant desire, the earnest aspiration, for a more holy and perfect life ; the looking constantly to higher powers for help to perform their daily routine of duties in the manner best calculated to produce happiness to all connected with them—and then, as they progress in spiritual development, the earnest wish to extend, by all the means in their power, this happiness to the whole human family. Such would be the desires of all properly influenced, and what harmony and love would reign on the earth if this feeling prevailed universally. The darkness that has so long enveloped all things in its gloomy mantle, would be removed ; light and joy would stream in from the higher spheres ; and a universal jubilant song of praise and rejoicing would rise from your earth, which now sends forth little more than sighs and groans of wretchedness and woe. Hasten, ye people, this glorious time! Let each one give his individual help. The work must commence within— self-examination, self-knowledge, is the foundation. Let this be done thoroughly in the first place, and you will be astonished what a flood of light will be the result. Instead of looking abroad to correct your neighbors, you will find you have plenty of work to do at home, before you look elsewhere ; and most likely, if you do it thoroughly, you will not, when it is completed, feel quite so much disposed to look after your neighbors. Thorough self-knowledge will lead to charity for the weaknesses of others. Seeing the multiplicity of failings and short-comings in yourselves, will naturally make you lenient to them ; and when this state of feeling supervenes, how much more kindly you will be disposed to them. I could say much more, but must withdraw for to-day.

L. D.

September 20, 1860.

ON GOD.

GOD in the spirit, and God in the human heart—the Almighty ruler of the universe—He who controls the heavens and earth, stills the raging of the tempest, and pours balm into the lowliest heart—He shall be the subject of our meditations this morning.

From the far West a voice arises : " Know thy God!" Know him, but in a far different manner than thou hast ever leârnt Him before. He is not the great unknown, incomprehensible, fearful being, striking terror and despair into the hearts of those who seek after Him. He is not a God of condemnation and censure, of punishment and revenge. He is a being to be loved and trusted in, to be looked to in our trials, to be made acquainted with our joys, to be thanked continually for blessings ; not to be entreated as a stern judge to share his rod. Punishments never come from His fatherly hand, they are the results of our own misdeeds. Everything that is for our advantage, comfort, pleasure, enjoyment, in this world—for our elevation, advancement and progression towards the next, is from Him. He rules our destinies, but only for good. He could not do otherwise. His nature is all goodness. How could evil, therefore, spring from it ? He is the light and joy of all things. If His beams are obscured by sin and sorrow, these are not of Him. He would have all happy, joyous and contented, and if they are not so, God must not be blamed for it. Nothing comes from Him but what is calculated to give help and happiness. He is the center from whom all goodness flows. Angels in the highest spheres, and the smallest insects, all derive from Him, the great source, their elements of enjoyment.

How, then, if such is the case, can God be a God of vengeance? It is a mistake, my friends, a fatal error in the creeds of Christendom, that has done more to demoralize the human family than any other. This is the great foundation of the doctrine of the atonement. The innocent man to suffer for a guilty world. Monstrous fallacy! How could such a doctrine obtain, as it has done, such prominent ascendency? Only minds warped and mis-directed, through fear of some invisible terror, could ever have been made to believe such a false and futile creed.

But, as I said in the commencement, a voice has arisen in these western lands, overthrowing with one sweep all such fallacies. Light has at length penetrated the dense darkness, and, through the ministry of spirits, the true character of God is more clearly revealed to His suffering world. By their aid, man can see for himself the true nature of God, can judge of Him from His works, and can love Him without fear or torment. Elevated by his contemplations of Him, he tries earnestly to come nearer His standard; he throws aside what debases and degrades him to the level of the brute, and essays a more pure and holy life—one more conformable to the teachings of his inmost sense of right. The Spirit of God in his own soul is aroused from its slumbering apathy, and goes forth to mingle with God's Spirit in all creation. He can rejoice with the timid flower, the humblest worm; all are partakers of the same spirit in degree, more or less, in accordance with the requirements of the individual entity.

When man learns to look upon God, in and through his works, he ceases to fear him. He sees for himself the love and wisdom that has designed and perfected all things, and he feels, when he commits a sin, that he is wronging the pure God Spirit within him, and that he must, from the nature of his being, suffer for his crime.

There has been much talk and argument lately as to the nature of God, whether he is a being possessed of form, or a subtile essence pervading all space? The angels, as well as yourselves, only know Him in His works. They feel Him around and in them, and they, in a far higher degree, enjoy the benefits of His providing; but no one hath seen God at any time—therefore none can describe Him. We, in our more developed state, can see more clearly, and realize more fully, His wisdom and love; but we, like you, have to look upward and around for proofs of His presence, and we conceive from these that there must be some great centre from which they emanate. Whether we shall ever be permitted to know more, I can not say. We are all contented here with the light and knowledge that we have. We are such constant recipients of His bounties, such joyous dwellers in the magnetism of love and wisdom He imparts to us, that we do not seek to penetrate into mysteries hidden for some wise purpose.

My friends, if God is the wise and good being I have endeavored to make clear to you, do you not see that goodness and wisdom should rule your actions, if you wish to be God-like? The more you can live in harmony with yourselves and the teachings of nature—the more simple, child-like, and unsophisticated by the trammels of earth-life—the more can this true light of the world enter into you, and make its abode with you. Call it spirit, angel, intuition, what you will, it is from the same source, the great fountain of love and wisdom —God.

L. D.

September 21, 1860.

ON HARMONY.

HARMONY, the music of the spheres, so little felt, so little appreciated on earth, how shall we sing thy praises to a world that knows thee not? How shall we enlighten mankind, and make them see thy many beauties? We, spirits who dwell in the regions of eternal love, know thee well, and long to make thy many charms manifest to the world.

Perhaps, if we explain fully in what true Harmony consists, men may be more willing to make its acquaintance. When they see the desirable results it can produce, they may make more strenuous efforts to cultivate the Heavenly guest.

Almost all men delight in music (earth music). It soothes, elevates, or excites, according to its nature. This love of melody shows that Harmony is inherent in man, undeveloped very often, but still there, ready to be called forth as circumstances allow it. So it is with our spiritual nature. The Harmony in that, *latent*, but still there, is ready to be called forth, not by the enchanter's wand, but by the influence of spirit-power over us. The true magnetism of good spirits can produce Harmony sometimes in the most discordant natures, and soften the most rugged dispositions. Often we see these miraculous effects, and, ignorant of the cause, wonder what has produced the change—why it is that the man formerly so overbearing and proud, who could not be gainsayed or contradicted, can now listen quietly and pleasantly, and without the ruffle of a feather, to the opinions of persons whom formerly he would not have deigned to give consideration or attention to for a moment. The Harmony developed in his

own spirit has wrought the change. *He* is free to act
and think as he likes, and he wishes others to enjoy the
same privilege.

So it is in other things. When all mankind have
learnt to desire the happiness of their neighbors as
much as their own, and seek to produce it by kindly
offices of good will, self-denial, patience and charity,
feeling that all have an equal right to the blessings of
this life, as all are of the same account and value before God—then, Harmony, something like the Harmony
of Heaven, may come down upon the earth ; music and
gladness will be in every heart, and joy and rejoicing
usurp the place so long occupied by sorrows and groans.
Every one can do something to produce this desirable
result, far more, indeed, than most people are aware of.

To develope Harmony, individual efforts may often
be the most telling. How frequently do we see one
Harmonious spirit (in the body I mean) work wonders
among a set of disorderly children. They cannot understand what makes them feel so happy, so kind, and
so tranquil. But it is all the effect of that Harmonious spirit working unseen among them. So it is
in more advanced life. While some men are as bad as
fire-brands thrown in our midst, others, calm and self-
possessed, sway with mildness and gentleness the wills
they come in contact with ; not seeking to bring all
into their way of thinking, but, after stating their individual opinions, leaving to their opponents the privilege of doing as they, in their individuality, think right.
And how often do you find that they have convinced
without effort, and harmonized while they have convinced.

I am not aware that any better method to insure
Harmony in domestic life can be pursued than this
mutual yielding up of tastes or opinions ; not that the
surrender should all be on the one side, but let each

18

have fair and equitable treatment. Where persons are
not unequally yoked together, the intellect of the one is
generally on a par with the other, and quite equal to
forming its own conclusions, and inharmony must result if justice in this is not observed. A woman is
generally more yielding, and consequently more Harmonious, than a man, and often smothers her own
opinions and conclusions, to prevent stirring up strife.
But I almost incline to think it would be better to
assert them sometimes, as no man has a chance to
develop fully into true Harmony who has not learnt
to listen and bear with the opinions of his wife.

These are some of the first steps to true Harmony ;
soon others will follow. When each is permitted to
assert their own opinions, they will exchange ideas on
an entirely different footing, and soon find that what
appeared to be wide differences in their views are
only imaginary distinctions—that iu reality they are
very much of the same way of thinking, and they will
then enjoy truly harmonious interchange of thoughts
and feelings, and love and peace will reign in their
bosoms.

Extend this feeling of mutual consideration further ;
let it obtain in the world ; let each man feel that he is
individualized, and is willing that his neighbor should
be so too. Then if he sees in him any little differences
in language, manners or dress, to what he has been
brought up to consider right, he will be willing to look
into the interior of the husk for the nut it contains, and
take and give all the good he can, never regarding the
unsightly covering which may oftener than he thinks
contain a royal jewel. He will then find that the harmonies of the spirit world will gradually develop themselves in his own soul, while he is not by unkind or
critical conduct destroying the harmonious feelings in
another's breast,

Harmony is the soul of bliss, the overflowing of the happiness engendered within by constant communion with higher sources of intelligence, and constant self-examination, lest we should intrude on, or wound the feelings of another, however humble or lowly. Harmony, to be true, must all spring from love in the soul, love to God, and love to man—a feeling of universal kindness; nothing can then ruffle or disturb its flow, no trial, no contradictions. Argument and opposition fall idly on the ear, penetrate no further than the surface, and cannot intrude on it.

As years pass on, this Heavenly calm and peace becomes more and more deeply imbedded in the soul. The approach of death, formerly so dreaded, is looked upon with equanimity, and the soul passes from its tenement of clay into its beautiful spirit-home without anxiety or fear—rather with joy and rejoicing.

L. D.

September 23, 1860.

ON PURITY OF LIFE.

PURITY of life, and purity of purpose, should be the aim of every person, but more especially of those professing Spiritualism. A new science, or a new creed, always leads men into critical examination of its views; and woe to that new creed whose members are found tripping.

It is hard for anything opposed to old prejudices and long established opinions to struggle into existence under the best auspices, but how much more difficult when its professed followers often disgrace its teachings by making them an excuse for sins and vices they dared not indulge in under the old dispensation. How much has this fatal mistake prevailed among the Spiritualists! They have many of them cast off the fear of hell, only, as it might seem, to set loose their vile, depraved natures. Thinking there is no eternity of punishment, they indulge every baser passion at will, and bring the beautiful and purifying teachings of true Spiritualism into contempt. Instead of being remarked for a morality and pureness of living without reproach, it is just the reverse. Every temptation is accepted; moral restraint is done away with, and they have only as it seems, to fancy some forbidden thing than they try to obtain it; for, as *they say*, nothing, not even another woman's husband, or another man's wife, is to be debarred them, if they choose to set their lustful eyes upon them, and can succeed in bringing them to the same way of thinking. It is true that many unhappy, uncongenial marriages are solemnized, and the parties would gladly separate; and better that they should do so at once than raise up families in discord and disunion.

But that is one thing, and the evil I complain of is another. Instead of freedom, it is licentiousness that animates mostly the persons who seek to disannul what has been too solemnly united to be so lightly considered ; and there is far more than meets the eye of the world in such arrangements. It is a pity that such things cannot be more thoroughly exposed ; that the anguish and misery, nay, even madness, sometimes resulting from these fearful doings, could not be known, that others, if similarly tempted, might take warning. But, what with the strivings of the miserable victims of desertion to hide their sufferings from the world, and the leniency with which the bulk of Spiritualists regard these crimes, little impression is made on the community at large by the most harrowing stories.

This cannot always go on ; a time will soon come when these wicked perverters of the holiest and purest doctrines ever given to man shall have a fearful reckoning. What if there is no literal hell of fire ? A hell will have a place in their bosoms, to the torments of which fire may be considered a trifle. The reproaches of their own consciences, kept back for a time, to return with tenfold force ; the silent anguish of the deserted wives or husbands, vividly depicted on their minds, the low degraded state of their own spirits ; the unutterable anguish of the darkness of desolation into which they must pass when they leave this body, might make the stoutest heart quail, could they for a moment realize it.

Many spirits have given many different teachings, some true, some far from it. As said in a former essay, "like attracts like," and liars draw liars to them. So with the sensual and depraved in other ways, all can find media to give what they wish—to make wrong appear right. But no more fatal teachings have come from these undeveloped sources than this, "That however sinful and vile a man may be, there is no punishment hereafter "—that all are better for the change called death!

My friends, it is not so—it is a fearful mistake. Punishment must be the award of the guilty; punishment, not from God, but still, punishment in the truest, most literal sense of the word. And there are none who will suffer more deeply, more lastingly, and find it more hard to rise from the bed of filth and anguish they are preparing for themselves, than the sensual and impure.

It is hard for me, my friends, to lay these unpalatable truths before you. I have struggled long with media to get them to you. They do not like to utter what is not pleasing and tickling to your palates. But it is necessary you should know and realize that you have been deceived by such teachings as I have been alluding to —that high and holy spirits could not give them—and that they are endeavoring in every way to undeceive you.

This medium has no fear of man before her eyes, and she mourns with a sinking of spirit, when she hears of the sorrows and miseries that are daily occurring from these sources, and from this cause I am able to speak boldly through her and tell you that immediate reform is absolutely necessary. You are injuring the cause you profess to serve more than you have the slightest idea of. If outsiders inquire from pure Spiritualists into its teachings, they are afraid to speak freely and enlighten them, as they otherwise would, for fear they should afterwards receive some of these debasing teachings from media, or get into communication with some other Spiritualists who may be a disgrace to the cause, and so disgust them with it; and still worse, furnish them with a handle against it to use among other enquirers. A follower of such a creed as Spiritualism should be pure as purity itself. No excuse should possibly be given for reproach or scandal. Every action should be guided by the rule of right. Love and kindness should reign in his heart for all. Purity and truth should be his companions. Then he could not blight and crucify the heart that trusted in him. He would want no medium to tell him he was wrong in such courses. His own intuitions would be his guides, and if his aspirations were pure and loving they would be never-failing ones. What if his companion were not quite the congenial mate he might devise? Influences could so work for him that he would never feel it. They could magnetize him to be happy and contented. If evil spirits can work so powerfully the other way, why should you doubt this? Have faith in your spirit friends. They can do far more for you than you have the smallest idea of, if you will only let them approach you as they wish. If, when you are tried and tempted, you lift up your hearts to them, (words are not necessary,) they can help you to resist; and after you have obtained one or two victories over yourselves and your tempters, it will be easy and simple for you to do so again. Soon they will leave you. When they find they have no hold on you, they will relieve you of their presence, and better and purer influences will take their place.

Hasten, each of you, my friends, this desirable result. Let individual efforts go forward, and soon we shall see a change in the whole bearing of Spiritualists. Instead of one part being afraid to come in contact with the other, because they dread the influences such persons may bring with them, there will be no shrinking of the kind. The dread of impurity keeps many good Spiritualists from coming forward at all, they hear so much to discourage them. But when this sin is removed from your midst, when the false mediums who have dared to advocate it, have their gifts taken from them,

(as they will have,) then you will see a change. Brotherly love and unity of the true kind, will reign among
you, and peace, harmony, and joy take up their abode
in your dwellings.

T. P.

September 24, 1860.

ON THE STATE OF THE DEPARTED.

My friend has asked us to give him our opinions on this momentous subject. It seems he has had some teachings that rather conflict with some remarks we made in our essay yesterday. Sorry are we to differ from other spirits in their teachings; but we must give the truth as we know it; if we do not, woe be upon us, as miserable perverters of the light and wisdom we are constantly receiving from the higher spheres. It is not often that we can give it as correctly as we would desire; but we are fortunate in possessing an instrument, at this time, who is willing to receive us as we come; to let her own mind rest in abeyance, that the truth may be more clearly made known to you. She is young in the business, and doubts herself; but we know what we are doing, and how well we can use her, and soon we will convince her that her own mind has no part in what we give through her. It is true our teachings have hitherto had her cordial assent, but she has no further part in them. This is a long digression, but it seemed necessary, for several reasons: One, to set the medium's mind at rest before we enter into our subject; another, to show our reason why we may differ from some others in our teachings on this subject. We will now return to our theme.

The state of the departed, immediately after death, has been a subject of deep consideration to many minds, in all ages of the world; but it remained for the Spiritualists of this century to throw the first certain light on the subject. They have learnt more than all the philosophers and wise men of their generation could conceive of. The spirit world, to them, is brought, as

2

it were, face to face ; they can talk with their departed, and can ascertain from them, with tolerable correctness, their present condition. They can even assist them to progress in their new state, or, reversing the case, they can receive assistance from those spirits to help them to develop here.

Such wonders as these could not have been believed by any one a few years since, and many more are yet in store, to be revealed to you as you develop, and are capable of comprehending them. But the future is not all one pleasant state of beatitude, where each one finds exactly what he likes best, just ready for him when he arrives there. Many, it is true, do pass on into happiness unalloyed, and far greater than their finite minds could imagine or comprehend ; but these may be considered the exceptions. Generally, man has left so much work *undone* in your sphere, that he is not prepared to pass on at once to these higher courts. The place would be distasteful to him ; the light and glory of them distressing ; and he would rather shrink away than remain.

There is a law in the Heavens that compels this. Where he has progressed to, there he must remain till his aspirations draw him up, little by little. If then, the comparatively good and moral man finds it so difficult to ascend into higher spheres, how must it be with the low and debased, the drunkard, the sensualist, the miser ? Would they be happy at all, think you ? Their occupations taken from them ; their bodies lost, and replaced by others, whose particles they cannot collect together ; rolling in darkness, incapable of any thing, some times not even of thought, while with others the thoughts are their most acute scourge ; every one having his own punishment, as he has wrought it out for himself on your earth plane !

This is the law that governs these things. You make

your own Heaven or your own Hell. The sins you
indulge in, produce such and such effects on your spirit
body ; in some, preventing its development at all, so
that the poor soul, when separated from its earthly
tenement, wanders, not knowing whither, and ages and
ages may be necessary to perfect that which might have
been so easily formed in beautiful proportions here.
No man sinks lower than the sensualist. He has so
debased the beautiful covering nature has endowed him
with, so contaminated it by the vilest usages, that it is
quite impossible any spiritual formation can be going
on while he is living such a life ; and it is most frequently such characters who find it the hardest to collect themselves and rise in the next sphere. But it is
difficult for all who have done wickedly in any way,
and even for those who have done *no positive wrong*,
but, having the means of doing good and relieving suffering humanity, neglected to do it, to make much progress at first ; so difficult, that higher spirits have taken
. the work in hand, and, through the media, who are
willing to help them in the work, are striving to reach
and help the undeveloped.

The friend for whom, or rather at whose request, I
write this, knows well how this work is accomplished,
for he has often assisted at such works of mercy, where
we were united together to raise poor unprogressed
spirits from their wretched condition. And this work
I would urge on the attention of all good Spiritualists,
and media especially, as by benefiting these poor unfortunates they prepare a band of grateful spirits to
assist *them* in *their* work, and also to return to those
dark regions from which they have been rescued, and
preach deliverance to other wretched captives.

In this way much good has already been done, and
many can testify to the gratitude the poor redeemed
ones have shown to their earth friends—following

them in their daily walk, and protecting them from dangers in a manner they are little aware of.

Another great good that media might effect, would be the relieving the world by degrees of the false teachings received from these unprogressed sources. Reform would spread rapidly if the spirits you redeemed could come and give their teachings ; and while they enlighten you as to the true nature of punishment hereafter, they would benefit the poor spirit listeners who always crowd around media to get benefited, but alas! too often are the worse for what they hear.

You may ask why they wish to speak through media when they know they are not giving truths. My friend, if you saw the condition of these poor creatures, you would pity rather than blame them. To stay with a medium is a relief and diversion from their gnawing agony when away, and they will give anything the medium or the parties may desire, only to be allowed to remain. They are quick and intelligent, very apt to catch up what they hear, and can retail it again in other words. They can, too, if you frequently attend their medium, read your mind far better than you have any idea of, and from that they can often give you a pretty good discourse, something that suits your taste, and harmonizes with your thoughts. Why should it not? They are your own thoughts retailed to you again. This is the way these poor unfortunates try to retain possession, and can we blame them? Rather let us try to redeem them, as I said, by our developing circles. If we succeed in rescuing twenty poor spirits from darkness, we provide a band of twenty earnest missionaries to go and preach to those spirits in prison ; and they can do far more, in proportion, than *we* can do through the medium. Spirits are not like mortals in this—they know that they are miserable, and they will gladly receive help from higher sources, and it is the highest

source of a high spirit's happiness to be able to assist
them.

Have we not said : " We will not cease from our
work while one spirit remains in darkness?" and will
we not keep our word ?

P.

NEW YORK, September 25, 1860.

ON HISTORY.

You may wonder, my friends, why I select this subject for our consideration this morning, and probably the views I express on it may not be very palatable to some of you, and quite new to others; but there is no subject that may not have some light thrown upon it by advanced minds, and certainly we in our sphere, who can look down on the history of all on your earth, may be supposed to have a good chance for forming our opinions.

We are not going to treat of History as a mere account of facts, but as more particularly showing the development of the human family. We wish to point out to you the impolicy of always referring to ancient records as guides for present conduct. Highly developed as the persons who wrote them must have been for that age, they were far below the developed minds of this century, both in their teachings and morality. Their standard was lower, their surroundings entirely different. Grossness, brutality and sensuality, in their coarsest forms, then met the eye. That these vices still prevail, I am aware, but they are not allowed to shock the public sense of propriety, as they did formerly. Students well know that some of the finest writers of antiquity were licentious in the extreme, and it is only recently that a cry has been raised against putting their tainted, polluted productions into the hands of your innocent children, as studies of *elegant classic literature.*

Such things could not be if men would think for themselves, instead of looking to the ancients to give them ideas. Is not every one endowed with a portion of God's spirit? Why cannot he call that forth, and

lean on his own intuitions? He would then have a
fountain of wisdom within himself, to guide and assist
him, and carry him up the hill of progression, far more
satisfactorily than the records of ancient days. They
suited the times they were written for, and did their
work. Now, let us pass forward for higher light and
farther knowledge.

When you have studied to weariness, and have learnt
all the teachings of the ancients by heart—Zoroaster,
Confucius, Christ, and a host of others—they all resolve
themselves into the simple teachings of the latter, that
" if you would be happy, you must be good ;" and to be
so, you must study, not books, but the happiness of your
fellow-creatures—" to do to others as you would they
should do to you." This is the golden rule ; all true
reformers taught this, as well as Jesus, and it is one of
the few teachings we have received from the ancients
that will never die out. If this were faithfully followed
there would be no further need of a Bible. Do you
not see how wide-spread would be its effects? All
know how *they* would like to be treated *themselves ;*
very kind and lenient, I am sure, they would be in their
judgments, very liberal in their donations, very atten-
tive in sickness, very patient, very forbearing. Reverse
the medal. Let them put their fellow men in their own
place, and act to them in the manner I have portrayed,
and what a world of harmony and peace you would
have! It would really be Heaven upon Earth.

Seeing this, my friends, what need is there of studying
these ancient records, of trying to understand the whys
and wherefores of every part? Why not let them sink
into the oblivion prepared for them, and press forward
yourselves, in your more progressed state, to higher and
more ennobling teachings? If the spirit of wisdom
could so enlighten the old fathers in those comparatively dark ages of the world, is it not as possible, and

quite as probable, that there are still greater stores of wisdom that may be poured out for you? Why burrow in the darkness of the past, when the present is teeming with light? Man, in his ignorance, thinks he knows all things. Alas! he knows nothing yet as he ought to know, and as he might know if he sought knowledge aright. But he studies the books of man's inditing, while true inspiration is waiting to be poured down upon him in all its fullness from the bright spheres above. What will all this earth-knowledge avail when you come into these higher spheres? So much more pure and lofty are our teachings, that all you bring with you will sink into insignificance, and you will wonder at your own blindness in wasting so much time upon it.

It must not be thought that we would advocate ignorant supineness, and indifference to the things of earth-life. Far otherwise. What we would say is this: The book of nature is a better study than old traditions, imperfect at the best, and filled with contradictions and demoralizing histories, which, you are taught, all came from the same inspired source. The Divine Being never contradicts himself. In the book of nature you can read of the wisdom and love that planned and directed, with so much intelligence, the organization of your earth and all others. It is a study that can never be exhausted, and from which you can gather new ideas daily. Then, can there be a better subject for your consideration than man himself? Can you read all the depths of the human heart? Has it not been said for centuries that "man is desperately wicked, born in sin, cannot think a good thought?" Now a light has broken in, and few, comparatively, hold to this dreadful doctrine. So it is; other errors and prejudices will gradually die out under the new light men will bring to bear upon them; and such should rather be the turn your inquiring minds should take, instead of wasting your energies in searching the records of the far past.

It is said that "distance lends enchantment to the view ;" I am sure it does to the characters of our old progenitors. Many of you would be very much disappointed could you see them as they were. They had like passions and failings with yourselves, just as liable to err—from pride, anger, and such like, and would not desire to be taken for models.

No, my friends, the best teacher man can have is the Spirit of God in his own soul. That will enlighten and guide him aright, if he will trust in it, fill him with true wisdom and true knowledge, and at the same time harmonize his whole nature. Possessed of this true light of the spirit, the cares and trials of life will not harrass and perplex as formerly ; true wisdom will show him that they are only for a season—that man's frown cannot affect him while the light of God's Spirit is in his soul. What are earth's gauds and toys compared to this ? Would you exchange this blessed glorious gift for them ? Would *you* put them in comparison for a moment ? No, my friend, *you* know better, you have not so learned of the spirit ; its teachings have gone too deep into your inmost soul, and you will be happy and blessed in possessing it, even were you stripped of everything you have been taught to hold most dear.

S.

September 27, 1860.

THE HAPPY.

THE happy are those who expect least, give most, and hold all things so loosely, as we may say, that they can resign them at any time without a murmur.

Such is a short definition of the meaning of happiness, but we will enlarge somewhat on the subject, and try to prove to you why it is so easily attainable, if men only took the right way to procure it.

If a man expect little he cannot feel unhappy if he receive little, and if he receive much his pleasure is enhanced by his expectations being surpassed. Whereas, the pleasure of giving from a full heart ungrudgingly, is well known by those who have tried it, to be far greater than the pleasure given to the recipients. But the truest source of contentment or happiness, lies in our holding all our possessions in trust, ready to give them up at any moment without repining. The same kind hand that gave has the right to take away. What have we that we did not receive? How then can we claim them for our own? If mortals would only bear these things in mind, how much misery might they be spared? If they would only feel that they are responsible to God and their own souls alone, and that they only can really judge them, how little would they care for man's opinions or man's frown? If the world look coldly upon them because they may not perhaps make quite so good an outside show as formerly, and even go so far as to censure and upbraid them because they may have been less successful in worldly matters than themselves, what effect would it have on properly developed minds? The peace and happiness they possess within would entirely blunt the points of such poisoned arrows. Magnetized by Holy Spirit, such remarks would fall on the ear without inflicting the slightest wound ; and however severe their worldly trials might be, they would still enjoy that happiness of which so many know nothing.

Happiness takes many different forms in the human mind. Some look for it in riches, some in love, some in this thing, some in that ; but true, lasting, real happiness, must come from the heart's being rightly regulated and harmonized to all things. Truly, the happiness of this world is not so unequally distributed as people think. The lowliest are often the most fully possessed of this treasure. Many a poor wanderer, the proud ones of the earth despise, possesses a bright and glorious spirit that will rise high in Heaven, when *they* may be grovelling in darkness.

There is far more real happiness among the poorer classes than people generally imagine. We spirits can come nearer to them to magnetize and help them in their daily toil. We can make them more thoroughly sensible of the enjoyment of a day of rest; and when the poor tired father, after his return from labor, caresses and pets his little ones, he feels a deeper sense of happiness than the rich can conceive of who have their children always around them.

Happiness, my friends, would soon be the portion of many on earth, if they would seek it in the right way. First, in making others happy, this is a sovereign receipt ; next, in so individualizing yourselves as to be able to stand unmoved amidst ruin of worldly prospects, or the censures of friends, (so called.) If you have done what you thought right to the best of your ability, and have not succeeded, why should you blame yourself, or allow the censures of others to have any weight with you ? If no one can reproach you for unjust, hard, or not strictly upright dealings, then is your soul right

before God and his angels ; and what are the judgments
of man in comparison ? They may depress and throw
a dark cloud over you for a time, but they cannot de-
stroy your inward peace. My friends, who have not
yet found this true happiness, let me urge on you the
importance of trying to obtain it as soon as you can.
Cast aside all selfishness, all pride in the gauds of your
earth-life, and strive to harmonize and sanctify your
spirits, that the true light from above may penetrate
them. You do not know what a dark wall you raise
around you by your contentions and strivings for earthly
distinctions. The bad influences that you stir up prevent good spirits approaching as they would gladly
do to help you.

Nothing is more adverse to the introduction of true
happiness among you than contentions in the family circle, where love and peace should hold the reins. One
inharmonious, discontented spirit is enough to disturb
the whole. Be careful, then, my friends, each one to
watch himself. Let no impatient word, no irritating
remark or unkind comment pass your lips. Be thankful each to the other for services rendered. Be lenient
in your judgments, never retailing unkindnesses or malicious stories, but if compelled to give opinions of persons, do so in the spirit of love, and always speak of
the good you know of them, and *let the evil rest.* This
is the true spirit of harmony—this is the true way to
be happy. But there are still other things that will
conduce very much to produce it. Charity to the poor,
and kindness to the sick are both great promoters of
happiness—not to yourselves alone—of course the benefited are happier too, and their prayers and good
wishes help to make a crown for their benefactors in a
higher sphere.

It may not, perhaps, be known to many of you, but
it is a fact, that when a person feels this true sympathy

for the suffering, their very presence is a benefit to the invalid ; a magnetism of healing power flows from them ; and if they are media, they are generally *led* to lay their hands upon them and can often heal them. These things are taking place daily in your midst, and more and more striking manifestations of this gift of healing shall be given, as the spirits can manifest through you. As sin dies out so will suffering ; as people reform their lives, their constitutions will be reformed, their children will be born healthy and well developed, and doctors and medicines will not be needed. Lawyers must also forgo their calling. When there is no inharmony and contention, there will be no need of them to regulate your affairs. Where every one is willing to do to his neighbor as he would be done by, what would be the use of a go-between? So when each man has the law of God written in his heart, what need of ministers with their large salaries and high looks, to teach it to you? All these things, my friends, must be done away with by slow degrees, but still, far more rapidly than you think for. Silently, but effectually, the transition is going on in men's minds, but few have the courage to declare it at present. The time, however, is not far distant when a great change will come over the world. Much of the inequality of social position will be done away with. Men will think for themselves and act for themselves ; rank, fashion, and all such artificial and hurtful distinctions will cease to bear sway over their minds ; they will look to themselves and not to others for guidance, and become individualized.

When this state of things shall prevail, then we shall find true happiness daily gaining ground among you. The *harmonies* of your natures instead of the *discords*, will become cultivated, and so entirely changed will man's condition become, that when the time arrives for his passage from this earth-sphere, it will be merely a gentle sleep, and he will scarcely realize it till he awakes in glory—for glorious will be the awakening of such harmonious and happy mortals.

N.

September 28, 1860.

ON THE POWER OF HOLY SPIRIT.

THE influence exerted over the human family by Holy Spirit coming direct from God into their hearts, enlightening their minds, guiding their paths, and keeping them in all their ways, shall be our theme this morning.

Men are too apt to look to themselves and intermediate agencies, for what comes in reality direct from God. There is no positive harm in this; at the same time, they would receive more of the fullness of the Spirit, if they looked higher for it. Angels and spirits all receive it from this same Divine source, and it is as freely offered to you as to them; but they, in their more enlightened state, can more fully appreciate this Divine Afflatus—they can realize more clearly the inestimable benefit conferred on them, and see and mourn the blindness of men in rejecting, or treating with indifference, their highest privilege.

How entirely, for centuries back, has this gift of Holy Spirit, promised so plainly and fully to the disciples by Christ, been omitted in the teachings of the churches; it is, indeed, completely lost sight of, both by preachers and hearers; and yet it was the highest blessing promised by Him to his followers before he left the Earth. He did not urge them to look for blessings from his death, but to wait for Holy Spirit, which he would send to them from his Father, God. And do you not remember how bountifully it was poured out upon them? How well that promise was fulfilled? Could they not do all things, under its powerful influence, that could tend to the furtherance of their mighty work? Did they not heal the sick—speak their Divine mission in diverse tongues to suit their various hearers? Many more were convinced by *their* teachings than even by their masters—this power of Holy Spirit was so strong upon them. So it was in those early ages of the Church. Why did it not continue? Why were such gifts allowed to die out? Did the sick cease in the land? Were all nations brought into harmony by the true light of their Gospel? Alas! no, my friends. Sickness and misery continued to exist almost as rife as ever, but men had commenced to quarrel about creeds and dogmas. Human authorities were set up, and Holy Spirit, which could and would have continued to guide them with as much and even more power than it had showered down in the days of the Apostles, was driven from the Earth.

Man in his blindness said there was no need of miracles after the apostolic age, and in that way reconciled the fact to himself, that Inspiration had ceased; but if he had looked more closely into the matter, he would have seen a very different reason why the gift of Holy Spirit had been withdrawn—he would have found that his own blindness and arrogant assumption prevented all chance of the Spirit manifesting. Quarrels on points of doctrine, immaterial at best, persecutions for conscience' sake, are fatal to Holy Influences. Where the true spirit enters, there must be harmony and love. Quarrels and contentions may bring in other influences, but they can never bring to their followers " That peace of God which *passeth understanding,*" the Bible says, but which we say, may be the portion of all who seek it aright.

This Holy Spirit, which has been driven from the earth so many years, Christ and his followers are again endeavoring to bring to you. The work is going on untiringly, unseen and silently, but without any intermission they labor for you. By tiny raps they first called attention to the unknown beings around you. Man had grown so worldly, so material, he had almost ceased to believe in the reality of spirits ; any one who professed to have faith in their existence, was looked upon as lunatic, or at least half-witted. How could they then reach you, since all were too worldly-wise to take them in their souls ? The bodily senses must first be appealed to, and unequivocal proofs of an outside intelligence be made plain to all inquirers.

Men began soon to make an examination into the phenomenon ; it excited attention ; comments of various kinds were made, and gradually, as more minds were turned to the subject, different and higher classes of manifestations became apparent.

But it is not necessary for me, my friends, to enter into further details of the phenomena of Spiritualism, with which you are no doubt fully acquainted. What I want to point out to you is this, that it is all for a wise and good purpose—that it has an end in view, as grand in its proportions as the commencement of Spiritualism was minute , trivial we cannot call it, for those tiny raps were the first beginning of a movement that will revolutionize the world. The Banner of Christ is raised on high, the Trumpets have sounded, and He with His angels have gone forth to the fight— a fight against sin and sorrow in all their various forms. The struggle may be long protracted, but He will be finally victorious over all opposition, both of men and spirits. Nothing can withstand Him. Strong in the power of God's holy Spirit, the hosts come on, armed for the contest. That which men drove from the earth so many centuries ago, when Christ first made it known to them, He will now establish in all its fullness, and a reign of true Celestial Harmony and Peace shall be the result.

Hasten this time, my friends. By your earnest efforts to further these desirable ends you can do much, more than you perhaps think ; but if you once receive this true light of Holy Spirit in your souls, you will do far more; your words will be words of power to convince others; your hands may carry a balm of healing for every wound; your hearts open and melting in charity for all, charity that not only relieves the indigent from bodily want, but follows out to the letter the teachings of the divinely-inspired Paul on this subject. Think, if all felt in this way, how differently the world would be constituted. Christ's mission would soon be accomplished, and Heaven and Earth rejoice together !

J. W.

September 29, 1860.

THE DAY OF REST—THE SABBATH DAY.

THE theme, my friends, selected for our meditations this morning, is one that has engrossed much attention, and on which many conflicting opinions have been given, and many stringent regulations to enforce their observance by the mass of mankind have been enacted. But it does not accord with the idea of freedom in thought, and individuality of character, that one man's mind should be the guiding rule of other men, or that one should be censured, and even punished, because he entertains different opinions on this to me open subject.

God has done all things well, and if he has constituted one man different to another, how can that other be judged by him? Let each man be a law unto himself. You may, perhaps, think that the utmost disorder and anarchy would prevail if such a rule obtained, but you are mistaken, my friend. In countries where the human being has had his mind, and sometimes his body, held in slavish thrall, some confusion might occur at first, but it would soon subside, and an increase of dignity and self-respect would manifest themselves in these degraded ones—while in countries where freedom of thought has made some progress in developing the higher qualities of human nature, still further and more and more rapidly will they tread the ascending scale. You may think I have wandered from my theme, but not so ; these preliminary remarks were necessary to lead you to the full understanding of our subject—the Sabbath day—a day that ought to be one of enjoyment and recreation to all—so seldom properly employed—so often miserably perverted to the most distasteful or unholy uses.

When God formed man and placed him upon this earth of yours, it was that he might be happy, and that after certain developments, necessary for his future progress, he should pass to still higher ones in another sphere. He did not give him any laws for his observance, but left him to follow his own intuitions, and develop as best he might. Soon man found for himself a way, as he thought, of being happier than ever—he would worship the Great Being who had created him, not with thanksgivings and songs of praise for His bountiful gifts to him, but with sacrifices and mortifying observances, to avert the wrath of a God who is all goodness and love. His own undeveloped nature had prompted him to the commission of acts which he felt were not right, and the intuitions implanted in him by God made him sensible of a something to come hereafter, for which he must prepare, and from which he dreaded that punishment of his misdeeds he knew enough to feel was his due. So it went on. As he developed in intellect, vices and crimes were committed, or rather those acts became vices and crimes which could not be considered in that light when man was so little elevated above the animal creation as he was at first.

When these actions had taken a definite character, and were recognized by the body of the people as evil, then they enacted laws to repress them, and religious observances to assist in preventing the evils so universally prevalent. Their wise men told them of an offended God, when they should have told them of moral laws offended. A day was appointed for the appeasing of this awful Deity. Sacrifices, sometimes of animals, but frequently of men, women and children, were offered up to appease the wrath of a God who is really all love, and wants to see His people happy. By slow degrees these casual observances took a more systematic form, and one day in seven was set apart for the worship of this unknown but dreaded power.

Such, my friends, was the origin of the Sabbath—sin, and fear of the punishment of sin! Little by little it grew into more notice, till its observance became universal, and now see what a stupendous fabric man has formed ; instead of the day being at his disposal, to do with as he sees best, man is the slave of the day! Let him feel it as distasteful and irksome as possible, outside ceremonies and quietude must mark its observance. Some there are who, going to the other extreme, make it a day of riot and drunkenness, but this only brings a further testimony in proof of its misunderstood character. The fact is, man should live every day as if it were a Sabbath. Every day he should be in that peaceful state of mind that it would not be out of place for him to commune in Spirit with God.

The human family has now reached a so much higher state of development than they had attained when the Sabbath was first instituted, that they may certainly be allowed to judge for themselves how they prefer to spend it. If a man sees no sin in a quiet walk, inhaling the odors of nature, and worshipping God in and through his works, can you, O fellow man, say he is wrong ? I say No ! however high your station in your church, your piety or your pretensions, that other men may find God much nearer to them in the field than you in your cushioned pew. Let each one be a law unto himself. As I before said, the institution of the Sabbath originated in servile fear, the offspring of ignorance and brutal sins. Why then should man continue to observe it, as he has so long done, with languid and cold services, from unwilling lips ? Rather let him so live that his daily life may be a perpetual Sabbath of rest and peace.   **M.**

September 30, 1860.

ON DEATH

THE subject that suggests itself for our consideration this morning has been prompted by one of those simple incidents daily occurring in your earth-life, united with so much that is painful and trying to human nature— the departure of a young girl's spirit to its new home —a home she has herself prepared for it, but which may be as widely different to any thing she has pictured as Earth is from Heaven.

Man little realizes the importance of understanding this momentous subject—he follows his daily avocations with zeal and earnestness, neglecting no opportunity of developing all the resources and talents in his possession to further his worldly schemes; while his unfortunate spirit too often languishes in darkness, utterly destitute of the nourishment it requires, and without which it cannot develop.

Does man forget that it is the spirit, and not the body, that is to live forever ? Does he forget that he brought nothing into this world with him, and that he can take nothing earthly away ? How can men be so blind to these things ? How can they wrap themselves up in careless ease and indifference about a future state, when they know that it will be forever and for-ever, that this life is only a short probation for that, and here they must make those preparations that may decide the destiny of their souls for ages ? We do not hold to the doctrine that punishment is eternal ; we know it is not. But there are punishments in a future state quite sufficiently severe to make man earnest to avoid them, if he rightly understood these things.

So many wrong teachings have been given to the

world on these subjects, that men have finally come to
the conclusion, as it seems, that it is the easiest and
pleasantest way to leave the matter at rest, so far as
their own individual efforts are concerned, and let the
priests do all that is necessary to ensure them a safe
entry into Paradise—money can purchase this, the
priests tell them, and money they give when their hour
of reckoning draws nigh. Money, their own idol, and
for which they spent a life of toil and privation, they
freely give, thinking through it can be done that work
it should have been the aim of their whole lives to
bring to perfection. Miserable, deluded victims of a
crafty priesthood, how are you deceived! What an
awakening is yours when the portals of the grave are
passed, and you enter that unknown Spirit-world!
There you will find a purgatory indeed, from which no
priest or prayer can save you—a purgatory from which
you might have escaped, had you only known how to
·act on this earthly plane. Had your spiritual teachers
taught you to work instead of pray, to cultivate the
higher nature within you, the God-principle implanted in
every man's breast—had they taught you to control yourselves, to love and help your fellow-man, irrespective of
degree or station, rather seeking out the debased and
vile as objects of your care, and doing to every one as
you would be done by—how different would be your
awakening in your Spirit-home! There you may now
find darkness and misery, solitude and bitter thoughts,
with no ray of comfort to beam upon you, nothing but
the reproaches of your own hearts to bear you com-
pany, all your own indulged passions tormenting you
without the means of gratifying them, cursing the
priests and the teachings that have brought you to this
fearful state—your poor soul is indeed in a place of
torment, and long may it have to continue there, unless
some kind spirit from the higher spheres can attract it

upwards. But the man who has done his work while on the earth, cultivating the interior principle, while not neglecting the body, who has fed his spirit with deeds of kindness and mercy, following in the footsteps and example of Jesus, self-denying, patient, charitable and full of love for his fellow-man, not merely relieving his bodily wants, but also nourishing his soul with Heavenly manna—he will find, when he enters on his new state of existence, what a beautiful Spirit-body he has prepared for himself—what crowds are waiting to welcome him and to see him clothed in it! All the poor afflicted ones that he may have relieved or soothed on their dying beds will be there—all the bright spirits who have aided and strengthened him in his daily walk will be there—these, and many others that he never knew, but who have watched his course approvingly, will welcome and conduct him to the bright and glorious home—the mansion he has prepared for himself in the Heavens!

Will not you, my dear friends, who read or hear these few words, look into this subject more closely than you have ever yet done? Will you not see the necessity of taking this work into your own hands? No priest, no prayer, can save you from your own evil deeds—in your own hands is the remedy. Cultivate your higher nature. Do not place your bodies, your most unworthy parts, in the seat of honor, and make them idols, but elevate your souls, that portion of God's nature implanted in all of you, and do deeds worthy of them. Let truth and love reign in your hearts, and universal benevolence guide your actions to your fellow-creatures. If such principles obtain among you, if this brotherhood of feeling and acting be established, your souls and spirits will grow together in beautiful proportions, and the change called death will be looked upon as merely an opening to a better life ; instead of being regarded, as it now is, as a thing of dread and horror, of which men dare not think, and on which they are afraid to look.

L. D.

October 1, 1860.

ON FORTITUDE.

THE ills of life are so numerous, and require so much strength of mind and true courage to support them, that I think we cannot do better this morning than devote a little time to the consideration of them ; and perhaps we may suggest some measures by which many may be alleviated, and some even cease to be evils.

First, then, let us consider what are generally looked upon as the great troubles human nature is liable to. Sickness, loss of fortune, and death, are three of the most prominent ; many more might be enumerated, but these three contain the elements of most others, and we will confine our attention to them.

The old Prophet says : " Man is born to trouble as the sparks fly upwards,"—but we say nay, we differ with the old philosopher *in toto*, and will not allow that man, or woman either, is necessarily born to trouble—that they meet with trouble only too frequently, I allow, but is not this generally caused by some outside circumstances that might have been avoided if the human family were following out a right principle of action ? Certainly it is. Man is living in a false position, and the sooner he rectifies it the better it will be for him, and the sooner will all these ills and trials of life, that so try his fortitude, cease to exist.

We have alluded in a former essay to a time to come when sickness will cease out of your land, when men will have so learned to live that their bodies shall be purified and sanctified—fit temples for the living God. Of course, when this moral perfection is attained, the purity of life it will induce will soon eradicate all the seeds of disease from their systems, and bodily sickness will be unheard of. This may seem a chimerical idea to some of you, and you will not, probably, live to see its fulfillment, but I think you will agree with me that all the diseases of your natures, both physical and mental, have been induced by neglect and abuse of the body and soul—originally created without any ailment whatever ; and when men only learn, as I said, to see this thing in its true light, and set manfully to work to cultivate health of mind and body on the true principles of purity and abstinence from all excesses, when they learn to be temperate in all things, pleasure, business, study, or whatever they have their minds turned to, they will soon see a wonderful change in their own health, and far more improvement in their subsequent offspring.

Loss of fortune we have cited as one of the trials of a man's fortitude, and it certainly is sometimes followed by most painful results, privations that the world never dreams of, but of which we spirits are too often cognizant, and which, when we can approach near enough, we do all in our power to soothe and relieve. But do you not see, my friends, that loss of worldly possessions ought not to produce these sad results if the world were properly constituted. If each man learned to hold his wealth as a trust given to him to do all the good within his power, if, living himself moderately and soberly, he used it to benefit and relieve others less fortunately situated, he never could experience these sad reverses. Where each one is willing to distribute of his surplus means to his poorer neighbor, when one who has possessed wealth is suddenly deprived of it, some other would be ready to supply his needs, and do for him as he had so long done for others. This is the law of retributive justice that should obtain on the earth, and of which angels are trying to show the advantage. Inequalities in the social plane always lead to more or less suffering. Where there are some inordinately rich, others are always to be found in the most abject poverty. More equal distribution of the good things of life would produce more happiness to both parties. Because people are immensely rich, it does not follow that they are happy; far otherwise, they have cares and anxieties, induced by their very superfluity of wealth, that the poor little dream of, and only too often is it the means of hardening their hearts, and making them callous to all the finer and more elevating feelings of humanity. Money and self are their only idols, and they have nothing to arouse them to a sense of their dangerous position till they find themselves naked in another state of existence, deprived of what they have so long worshipped, and with remorse alone to supply its place! The sufferings of the poor from this unequal state of things, I need not dilate upon; you all know more or less of what they must be. The exposure to hunger, cold and nakedness, so often presented to your sight by your poorer population. must make you well acquainted with some portion of their misery, and if you visited their dwellings you would see much more. But I will not enumerate their trials; all of you can see for yourselves what a benefit to them would be some of the surplus wealth locked up in the coffers of the rich—how advantageous the more equal distribution of the blessings intended by a wise Providence for all alike.

Death, the last trial of all, we have shown in former essays would be looked upon as anything rather than a trial, if men lived as they should do, and understood as they might the true nature of that change. Soon, I trust, this light will burst upon their souls—that true wisdom from above that will show them the vanity and folly of laying up treasures for themselves upon earth, either of money or pleasures of a perishable nature.

Pleasures, improperly indulged in, lead, as we have shown, to sickness, and, we may add, deformity in all its forms, and it is only by thorough reformation in the lives and actions of mankind that these curses can be removed.

In regard to the distribution of their wealth, I am afraid I have a still harder task to prove to them the necessity for it. But, my friends, it is only when this state of feeling exists, when men are ready to do good, willing to distribute—when these teachings are really lived out upon the earth, that the last great trial of your life can be deprived of its sting, all fear and doubt be removed, all gloom and terror done away, and death be welcomed as a friendly messenger to carry you to realms of bliss and still higher progression.

N.

October 2 1860.

ON LOVING THE WORLD.

LOVING the world, and the things of the world, has been the great drawback to all Spiritual progression. When men's hearts are set on these things, their great aim will be to attain them, and if they cannot succeed by honest industry as fast as they would desire, too often they resort to other and less fair methods. I have watched the progress of many Spiritualists, and frequently found that after a commencement of pure and unalloyed faith and joy in the manifestations vouchsafed to them, that though satisfied with the knowledge that their departed friends still exist and can interest themselves in the future progress of their earthly relatives, they seem, after a time, to find this knowledge insufficient, and instead of trying to develop still higher and more ennobling teachings from their Heavenly visitants, their worldly feelings step in, and they seek in all manner of ways to turn the spirits to account for mundane purposes. Spirits of a low grade may endeavor to assist them, or may profess to do so, but it is a dangerous business for any man or woman to rely on their help—they may prove more delusive and fatal than the *ignis fatuus* that beguiles the lonely wanderer into the swamps of your Earth. High and holy spirits do not come to you for any such purposes ; they are too far-seeing, too much progressed, to give aid in such matters. In his Earth-life man has his own appointed duties to perform, and he has mind given him to direct him and guide him in the performance of them. How can he become individualized if he relies on other powers to think and work for him ? And what is still more detrimental to his progression, he sometimes looks to them to supply his needs, and bring him money. Be assured, my friends, when spirits do these things (for I do not say they cannot, though not after your earth-fashion,) they are low and very undeveloped beings you call to your aid, and bitterly will you repent having used such instruments. If men were not so worldly, how much higher might they rise—how happy and pleasant would this life be to them—simple in their tastes, simple in their pleasures, they would require so much less to supply their necessities that they would not have nearly so much temptation to do wrong as they now have. The spread of luxury and extravagance is become one of the crying sins of the land, and must, unless checked, lead to untold misery. When vices come to a certain point a sudden check is put to them from unseen sources, and woe to that land that draws such punishment upon it.

No nation has seen more prosperous times than this one, no people have made such rapid strides in progress —but let them not abuse the gifts so bountifully showered upon them, lest darkness and desolation overspread their fair country. The same hand that gave can take away, and if vice and immorality, luxury and extravagance, fraud, chicanery and deceit, are allowed to continue on unchecked in your midst, while the poor and wretched starve unpitied in your streets, a severe day of reckoning will come, and soon will the voice of lamentation and wailing take the place of music and revelry that now tickles your ears and delights your senses.

I commenced by speaking of the manner in which the Spiritualists so often injure themselves, and the creed they profess to believe in, and I would say a few more words to them before I close these remarks.

Spirits, my good friends, like mortals, are liable to err—the lower ones are far from perfect, as you may suppose, and if they deceive you by false promises and expectations of wealth, or knowledge, or station, which they know will never be attained, you must not blame them too much; rather censure yourselves who have craved such things from them, and which they, knowing your desires, have done their best to gratify. We have told you before how anxious all undeveloped spirits are to remain around a medium, and (if they find a chance) communicate with mortals—of course, when they do so, they say those things that they think will be most pleasing, and draw the man or woman to their medium again for further information.

To the Spiritualists who have no higher aim than prosperity in their worldly affairs, by fair means if they can, but prosperity at any rate, I can say no more—deceived they are, deceived they will be to the end. But to the truly inquiring and earnest truth-seeking man who wishes to know the right, and to do it, I would add this advice: Shun all mediums who touch upon these things. Spirits cannot know as well as yourselves how your worldly affairs should be conducted. How should they? They are not gods! And if you can so live as to find true spiritual knowledge coming to you through your own mediumship or intuitions, you will be far happier, and far more likely to possess the truth in your soul than in any other way.

L.

October 3, 1860.

ON CRIME.

WE have chosen a subject but little understood,
though much spoken of, for the theme of our meditations this morning, and we hope to be able to dictate
to our medium some remarks that may be beneficial to
the world at large. Men in all ages have felt the
evils that resulted from the commission of what they
called crimes ; they have known that there must be
something wrong in the workings of human laws and
ordinance, that in defiance of all man's regulations
crime still continued in all its dark deformity—life
sacrificed, vice indulged in, oppression and tyranny
ruling, where the teachings of Christ and His followers
had been promulgated. I do not, my friends, say anything of the followers of other creeds (the difference in
the amount of crime is not remarkably in favor of the
so-called Christians, however). I speak more particularly now of the Christian sect—they who, having the
purifying teachings of Jesus for their guide, still follow
after their own desires, and indulge every base and low
inclination. How is this, my friend? Can you explain to me why men with enlightened minds, having
the true way of holiness and purity of life so clearly
pointed out to them, fall into these gross sins, without an
effort, it would seem, to save themselves ? Would you
not suppose that they would rather choose that higher
life that they are told will bring them into harmony
and peace? Yet it is not so, except in rare instances.
As a general thing, men choose darkness rather than
light. This shows very clearly to us spirits that the
one is preferred to the other. Their natures have become so depraved from contaminating influences, car-

ried through many generations, that they are not able, without some outside assistance, to struggle against these feelings. The sins of the fathers are literally visited on the children, and they in their turn convey to their posterity still further evil. Man cannot wrong his own nature without defiling it ; if he indulge in licentious pleasures, scrofula and its attendant ills must descend to his posterity—if his brutal appetite for blood and rapine bears sway, like passions and tempers will obtain in his offspring ; true, they may not show so perceptibly in the next generation, but the seed is there, and will develop itself in time. I might go on specifying, but it is enough for you to know how this thing works ; you can now trace it out in all its bearings for yourselves. You will then see clearly what it is my aim to show you, namely : that crime is a necessary consequence of indulged passions, it needs no outside influence to prompt to the commission of it (though there are undeveloped spirits only too ready to lend their aid). The mind to do is in the man himself, ready to act when occasion serves.

Having now shown you how it is that crime still rules supreme, in spite of the teachings of reformers in all ages, and in defiance of your most stringent laws, do you not think you can see for yourselves a more excellent way to eradicate its poisonous and death-dealing influence from the Earth ? Do you not see, my friends, it is a work every man must do by himself ? And first of all, the labor must be in himself. If the sins of the fathers have descended to the children, either in the form of sensual desires, avaricious craving, blood-thirsty and revengeful passions, pride, disease, untruthfulness, dishonesty, or any other vice that degrades or causes him to err, let him faithfully strive for the eradication of that evil—let him purify himself from that passion or sin that does so easily beset him, and he will not only feel the blessed effect of his work in his own life, but his unborn offspring will have still greater cause to thank him. They may not be quite freed from the taint, but it will have slighter hold, and in the succeeding generation it may die out altogether.

We have spoken above of those characters not utterly depraved, as you term it—those who have still a moral sense within them that would urge them to reform themselves if they would listen to its teachings. But there are multitudes of others that must be helped, in this reformatory movement, by kind and sympathizing mortals and spirit-friends ; they have fallen too low to rise by their own efforts. In many instances it would take long to convince men of the necessity of a change, they are so wedded to their sins and blinded to the truth ; but spirits have patience, and bide their time to work upon them with most effect, but they need also the co-operation of mortals to help them effectually. If they can once instill into the minds of the human family the importance of this movement, the necessity there is for them to work heart and soul, and, striking at the root of all evil, eradicate it from the earth (as with the assistance of their spirit guides they surely will do in time), there would no longer be this necessity for laws and law-givers, and the redeemed from sin and suffering would be a law unto himself. Crime would cease to be known among you ; love, wisdom and harmony would reign in your breasts and angels come and take up their abode with you.

N.

October 5, 1860.

ON CHARITY.

CHARITY—the mission of angels to men is more especially to enforce the practice of this truly God-like attribute—this emanation from Deity—this motive power to redeem the world from all misery, sin, and consequent wretchedness. How shall we sing its praises? How shall we inspire you, my friends of Earth, with the full realization of its manifold beauties?—with that living abiding sense of its presence in your hearts, that it may rule all your actions, guide and govern your thoughts, and make you, while living on your Earth-sphere, fitting companions of angels, and recipients of their highest teachings?

Very fully has Paul, our friend and co-laborer, entered on this subject; plainly and concisely, and at the same time fully, has he described its bearings on the human family, if properly carried out. But, my friends, the Christian world, who hear that sublime chapter of Corinthians read, are become so accustomed to the poetical and harmonious jingle of the words, that the sense rarely makes any impression on their minds, and as to *practicing* its teachings, they look upon that as too entirely out of the question to enter into their calculations for a moment. The idea of such utter self-abnegation, such extended and universal love and charity as is there enforced—the forbearance under injuries, the returning kindness and good service for contumely and scorn—all these things are so far beyond the scope of their Christianity (as they call it) that they do not in their hearts believe it was ever intended they should put it in *actual practice.*

And yet, my friends, what else could have been the

object of those teachings, and what motive could **Paul,** or any other of the apostles have, in enforcing these great truths upon the world? Did they not receive them direct from higher sources? Were they not as far above and beyond Paul in his natural mind as they have always been beyond the people for whom they were written? Certainly they were. But is it always to be so, my friends? Are you never to develop up to them? Is this world to go on, age after age, progressing in everything that man deems worthy his attention, and is this sublime and holy doctrine of love and charity never to bear sway among you? Are you to go on forever fighting, murdering, persecuting, slandering, reviling, and despising, as the case may be? Are fraud and oppression to prevail always, and the poor and down-trodden never to cease in your land? My brethren, these things should not, could not be, if charity, divine and heaven-born charity, prevailed among you. If each one looked upon his neighbor as a brother, and treated him as such (and you know, my friends, all are your neighbors in the Bible-meaning of the term), how differently would this world be constituted and governed! The law of love ruling would obliterate the law of fear altogether.

Let us suppose, for a moment, a nation ruled by kindness alone—the teachings of Paul carried out to the letter—beginning with the highest in the land, how would he act? Would he require the servile homage of his fellow-man? He could not receive it. If all men are brothers, why should he use his brother worse than himself? The same holds good in regard to war and conquest. Could a king or ruler make war upon his fellow-man if he had the true light of love in his soul? No, my friends, he could not do these things, or any others that would militate against the happiness of his fellow-creatures ; and this rule working through all ranks and conditions, would produce like beneficial effects in all ; gradually the condition of things would change for the better, by distributing more equally the comforts and necessaries of life. A brother having abundance could not then see a brother in want ; he must relieve suffering wherever he finds it—and were all to follow this Heavenly rule, how soon would the ills that now afflict your beautiful world die out !

I have shown you in a previous essay how sickness may be removed altogether ; I now show you how poverty, war, contentions, and all unhappiness, may follow in its train. You have suffered too long already, my friends, from these causes ; it is time for you to take the field in earnest, and relieve yourselves from their burden. · The remedy is in your own hands ; the work lies within ; no one can do it for another, to your own conscience you must stand or fall ; examine yourselves carefully, and see in what you fall short of this true charity and brotherly love. Do not look into your neighbors' souls, but into your own ; commence the reformation there, and show by your actions how truly and fully this God-spirit is working in you. Some few there are in the world who have in true earnestness followed out these teachings to the best of their ability, and they find that the more they strive to do so the more power is given them to persist, and the more true peace and good-will for man, their neighbors and brothers, in the real meaning of the word, is added to them. Daily they find new paths opened to them to harmonize and assist, and they go on in their work rejoicing. My friends, why cannot I see more of you following in their steps ? Why is it that, instead or this brotherly love, contentions and strife are in your midst ? Why is it that jealousy and ill-feelings obtain in your meetings, so that even spirits are brought into the arena to fight for you ? Is this as it should be ?

Is this the true light, think you, that shall enlighten a world ? My friends, my friends, think on these things —think, before you are too far gone astray, if such could be the true teachings Spirits have left their bright homes to bring to you. Better we had never come, could we do nothing more than give such teachings as you too often receive from sources too low and debased to be listened to for a moment. But we cannot enlarge on this subject now, another time we may take it up. We have already alluded to it on a former occasion, and we will enter into it more in detail by-and-by. At present our medium is tired, and we must conclude. We will only add, that if you follow out the teachings we have been enforcing, heartily and fully, there will be no more wranglings and strife among you, and no evil or malicious spirits will come and lead you astray by their false teachings. This law of God in your souls will keep you pure, and no impure spirit or spirit teachings can come nigh you. Farewell, my friends ; in love and kindness I take my leave now, let me not have to come again in wrath.

J.

October 7, 1860

TRUTH is a subject we have chosen for our theme this morning ; it is made a constant subject of conversation among the people of the world, and many are truly anxious to understand it in all its bearings, for they know enough to see that truth, in its extended sense, means far more than the literal affirmation of a fact.

Truth is the life-giving principle of all things. If there is no truth in what we communicate to you, then there is no vitality in our teachings. True spirit communion brings with it a life and power to work in and through the persons receiving it, not only for their own benefit, but for all with whom they come in contact ; they feel the living principle of these things, and they are anxious that others should enjoy the same blessing.

This is one way that truth works; another is in endeavoring to discover the secret things of the Lord ; things said to have been hidden since the formation of the world, but which the truthful and earnest seeker now sees a chance of understanding ; he dives deep into the mysteries of the creation ; he traces things to their source, and finds truth and beauty combined together to form a harmonious result, which he now sees far less difficulty in comprehending. The truth becomes more and more perceptible the farther his researches extend, and he retires from his labor satisfied with the result, and glorifying and praising God, whose truth and wisdom are so manifest in His works.

Again, truth is often something which you may fully comprehend, but at the same time find it exceedingly difficult, nay, almost impossible, to make clear to the mind of another ; organization, prejudice, education, and many other things, may make it quite impossible for them to receive it, while with you it is a, positive certainty. In regard to religious belief—can there be any subject named on which there are greater diversities of opinion? Yet each one is right, to his own mind—the creed he holds is the truth to his soul, and he lives and dies by it ; can he give a greater proof than this of the sincerity of his faith in it ? Of course we are now speaking of sincere inquirers, not of those who have never gone far enough into the depths of their own spirits to care whether they have truth or the reverse. .

But truth must be brought nearer home to every man and woman than all this. Abstract speculations and creeds are all good in their way, and tend to elevate the weak, or amuse and instruct the inquiring mind. Truth, in its practical bearings on the human family, must be the vital, living principle within that can control all their actions, elevate their desires and aspirations, and render them responsible to their own higher natures for any deviation from its paths. With truth reigning supreme, how much would the aspect of things change to the human family ! What might formerly have made no impression on their obtuse natures, would, with this intelligent monitor within (quickened and elevated to his rightful post) appear vile and discordant to their more elevated conceptions. Lies, formerly indulged in without restraint, could not be tolerated, and far more widely than this would the reformation extend—an acted or quiescent lie would be equally distasteful to them ; the purity of truth would rule their language and their lives, and they would dread and shun what could mislead or contaminate.

My friends, let this principle of truth extend still

66

further; carry it with you in your researches after spiritual teachings; let no desire for wealth, station, success in worldly projects, or any other thing, accompany you in your seekings for truth through these sources. Pure in spirit, and truthful in your desires, go to your Spirit-friends,, and if they can they will help you with their counsels; they may not be able to give you all you need at first, but if they find you patient and truthful they will not willfully mislead, and gradually you will draw higher spirits to you. No poor spirit will willingly debase himself; if he does do so, it is because he would not be received if he came in any other way. Media and Spiritualists are far more to blame for the false communications they receive than the world has any idea of—they want what they get. Do you ever hear of *really* pure-minded women being insulted by the licentious and degrading free-love doctrines so continually given through some mediums? Do you ever hear of men who are really pure being told that they may indulge their passions in any way, and that it is good and necessary for them? No, my friends, these teachings come from, and to, those who seek for them; and no matter what any one may say to you to the contrary, I affirm that mortals, and not spirits, are to blame for them. I have told you before how spirits want to progress; they come for light, and when they cannot get that, they will do these things for the mediums, so that they may stay around. But are they to be blamed? Rather, I think, blame the untruthful money-loving mediums, and the base seeker of such encouragement to continue in his sin.

Truth, my friends, must ultimately prevail; all this wrong will be done away with—and, in the meantime, let me say a few words to encourage true media and truthful seekers to persevere. Be assured, my medium friends, you who have devoted your lives and talents to this work in all truthfulness and sincerity, that no false or bad teachings shall come through you, if it is (and we know it is) in the power of good spirits to prevent it. *We* will guard you, and your own truthfulness will guard you also. Do not fear man's judgment. If your teachings should be contrary to what has generally obtained, be satisfied—you know your own hearts, your truthful desires, and let no man's opinion have power to move or disturb you ; all will come right at last, and we can sustain you through harder trials than these. And to the truthful seeker I would also say some words of comfort. Be not discouraged if you meet with conflictions, and doubts arise—seek out the cause of them, and then avoid their recurrence. Many media have many minds, and many minds have many spirits round them, therefore be very careful who you select to take your communications from ; and when you have found one on whom you can rely, do not run after others and try to prove or disprove what you have got through them ; there is sure to be confliction if you do. No two are alike ; one can not enter on the plane of the other at once, if at all—then how can they vouch for the correctness or reverse of what you receive ? But the most sure way to obviate all difficulty is, to try and develop your own soul, so that there is no need to go to mediums at all. Spirits can teach you far more satisfactorily in this manner, and by degrees you will acquire a fount of living waters within yourselves that will never fail, and will lead you on unto everlasting life.

We have not been able to say all as clearly as we could wish on this subject—the interruptions have been so numerous, and the medium not very well ; but we have stated enough to show you that truth has a

far wider meaning than the world generally attaches
to it, and that if you wish to progress in Spiritual or
any other knowledge, truth must be the basis on which
to place yourself, and the only thing that should satisfy
a sincere inquirer.

October 8, 1860.

ON SOBRIETY.

SOBRIETY, in all things, should be the aim of every man; not only in things pertaining to the appetites and passions, but also in the use of our reasoning and intellectual faculties. A man may be as intemperate in his pursuit after knowledge as in the use of alcoholic drinks, and it may be equally injurious to him physically. Moderation in all things is the law to be observed, if you would wish to preserve physical health and harmony of soul. To obtain this desirable result, man must follow the law of reason, implanted in him for this very purpose. What is he different from the brutes but in this faculty of the soul? and if he does not use it, does he not bring himself to their level?—we could not show to them the impropriety of overtaxing a brain or overloading a stomach; and one might almost think some men were quite as unconvincable, from the repeated lessons they receive, and the little effect that results from them; but they must know, if they will only think for a moment, that both brain and stomach are too delicately organized, and too much in sympathy with each other, to be either of them imposed upon without disturbance to both. If the brain is the over-worked laborer, dyspepsia. paralysis, and all the nervous diseases, manifest themselves; the liver refuses to act, the bowels to perform their functions. In fact, there is no end of the enumeration of ills we might specify from these inordinate draughts on the mental faculties. While on the other hand, intoxication and gluttony result in obesity, imbecility, and finally apoplexy or delirium tremens. So you see, my friends, though the kind of intoxication may be different, the results in both cases are equally bad. One is not indeed so degrading to the man, but it is equally certain in its effects ; both lead to premature decrepitude and death, and both should be carefully avoided, if you wish to fulfill your allotted duties in your generation.

You are apt to look upon the drunkard with contempt; you say : " Why does he not exert his moral courage and resist the intoxicating drink.?" My friends, the same moral courage you find it so easy to recommend to his practice, should be exerted in your own case when *you*, led away by a fascinating study, or some new science, pursue it into the midnight hours ; daily you continue your researches; some new light seems to dawn upon you ; more and more eagerly you follow it up—exercise, food, family ties, everything, is thrown aside by, and for, this one engrossing pursuit ; after a few hours' broken and unrefreshing sleep, you rise again to pursue the same course. Day after day this may continue—with some, who are strongly organized, month after month—but it cannot continue always ; the neglected and abused organs of your body will make themselves heard at last ; they may have muttered unregarded during some time, but there must come a final crash, when they will fail to do their allotted work, and the machinery being brought to a stand still, paralysis or something worse may surprise the unwary mortal.

And now, my friends, say if you think the student, as I have described him, has any more moral courage than the drunkard. I think not; he follows after what he prefers, without any reference to what it may cost him— he cannot give it up, even when he feels that it is killing him, and why? Because he likes it. Does the poor inebriate do any worse? I think the latter is more excusable, for as he goes on from bad to worse, his moral faculties are deadened, while the suicide for knowledge is more clear-headed and far-seeing daily. Do not, however, mistake me, or put a wrong construction on my words ; far be it from me to excuse or palliate the sins of gluttony or drunkenness ; the evils resulting from these vices are too wide-spread and well known to require me to say a great deal in explanation or reprobation of them ; where all see so plainly the necessity of combatting and overcoming them, the work is already half done. But intemperance in the pursuit of knowledge is less suspected, less guarded against. Men are apt to think they are doing a good work, enlightening their own minds that they may benefit others from their fount, and so get carried away beyond the bounds of reason and prudence. True wisdom would show them that knowledge without health, and consequently without harmony of spirit, could not be the right kind to make them happy. And after all, my friends, happiness is the end and aim of their researches. Happiness is what all are striving to obtain ; very different are the methods by which the human family are working for it, but still that is the object of their varied labors ; some few find it, some few know what it is to enjoy perfect contentment and peace here on your earth ; but the majority are widely removed from it, and will continue to be so while they take such erring guides to show them the way to its attainment.

This world of yours is full of good and beautiful gifts to man, from an All-wise source, and all are to be enjoyed in moderation—not one alone, or two, or even three, of these gifts, to the exclusion of the others, but all (as they were intended) be brought to conduce to his happiness and comfort. As the human body has many functions, and each function is necessary and should be exercised to make harmony of the whole, and form a perfect man, so the material world has many functions, many means of developing in man the higher and more spiritual parts of his nature. Can he walk abroad in the fields in the glorious sunshine without feeling exhilarated and benefited, physically and morally? Does not a glow of gratitude and love go up to the giver of this healing warmth of the sun, this cooling magnetism of the earth? In inhaling the fresh breezes he derives strength, in the cooling shade of the trees refreshment—the birds singing in the air, the sportive animals playing unconcernedly around him, all would contribute to produce a feeling of refreshment and repose to the mind rightly constituted to enjoy them; and to vary his pleasures, let him visit the abodes of the sick and suffering ; let him impart to those poor sinking brothers the words of wisdom and love he has learned in his walks, with Nature for his companion and teacher ; let him soothe them with the thought of how much they really have, poor and miserable though they may be, that poverty cannot deprive them of ; relieving their bodily necessities to the extent of his ability, point out to them the happiness that may be enjoyed here, even under the most discouraging circumstances, where they can look up to God with a thankful spirit for the air, the light, the sun, the rain, the night, the day, the summer, and winter. Everything in Nature, outside of man, is theirs ; man cannot deprive them of these blessings, and the richest can derive no more benefit or pleasure from them than the poorest. Is not this a thought to make glad the heart? And then in addition, to be able to tell them of Spirit friends, their constant watch over and care for them, their sympathy in their sufferings, their constant effort to relieve and cheer them when most desponding, and the certainty that when their trials are over here they will be waiting to receive them into their happy home. Is not this a mission of happiness to the giver and the receiver also ? Should you not, think you, feel better after it? Would your souls and bodies both harmonize? You may be a little fatigued, and your purse may be lighter, but it would not be a fatigue to kill, and your brain or stomach (for I am addressing both kinds of intemperates) would be rested and refreshed ; the former invigorated to pursue its studies, and derive more benefit and more enjoyment from them.

Think of these things, my friends, and I am sure you must agree with me. Enjoy all the blessings you have so bountifully received—let each one have its allotted place. Exercise, physical and mental, is equally necessary, but do not let exercise exclude other things. There is plenty of time for all, if men will use it aright —a time to work and a time to play. Let each have its fair proportion ; one is quite as necessary as the other.

We have extended our essay farther than we intended, and our medium is tired ; we therefore take our leave, trusting you will take the subject we have treated on, into your earnest consideration—remembering that though we have only spoken of two kinds of intemperance, a man may be intemperate in any and every pursuit he carries beyond the bounds of moderation, and allows to encroach on other duties.

N.

October 9, 1860.

ON LOVE.

PAUL says, "Love is the fulfilling of the law." What law? The Mosaic, or the Christian, or any other specified and written laws? No, my friends; the law of love is the law of God—the kind and benevolent feelings implanted in our hearts by his Holy Spirit, coming direct from him and returning to him with added beauty, as it manifests itself in us. I say in us; for we, like you, are the recipients of this God-principle—the only difference is in degree; we can receive it more abundantly; this holy and ennobling love, so constantly pouring out from the Great Fountain of all goodness, is freely bestowed on those who seek it aright; none are forbidden to take it in all its fullness and enjoy its blessed and comforting influences. Filled with this love, a man feels in harmony with all persons; circumstances, trials, contentions, sorrows cannot move him to contend or to despond; he is impervious to the darts of the wicked, or to the attacks of the malicious. You may say, "I have never felt this love; I am depressed by this thing, cast down by that; troubles and doubts overwhelm me, and I even debate within myself, whether I am better or worse for my knowledge of Spiritual things." My friends, doubts would not arise if you had sought these things out in the right way; if you had taken hold of the matter by the roots, in your own hearts, and cultivated there this true love—principle, examined yourselves thoroughly, and ascertained faithfully, if there were any shortcomings in your own actions, that might prevent, for a time, the entrance of it as an inmate of your bosoms. If a man is in harmony with himself, everything ap-

pears bright and lovely to him ; he can sympathize
with the mirthful, or he can comfort the afflicted from
his own harmonious stand-point ; he is so filled with
this feeling of peace and joy, that he seems to tread
on air; nothing disturbs his equanimity, and he wants
every one he comes in contact with, to feel as happy as
he does himself.

Such is the state of mind we would wish to establish
upon Earth ; such the feeling this love would induce
among men, if they would only receive it freely, as it
is freely offered to them. The task of harmonizing
themselves, so that it could constantly dwell with
them, would not be so difficult, if they set to work in
earnest, and we, their spirit friends, would be always
near to assist them in their efforts ; the more they
try, the more we can do. Every wrong feeling, every
inharmonious or unkind thought conquered, brings us
so much nearer. Day by day as one stubborn or unholy passion is broken up, we silently draw closer,
baptizing them with this heavenly magnetism, and fill-
ing the space in the soul, hitherto profaned by these
bad influences, with love, and peace, and joy.

This love " that passeth understanding," simply because men rarely live so as to understand it, is not so
difficult of attainment ; it is within the reach of every
one of you, and is the truest foretaste, when possessed,
of the life hereafter. Will you not, my friends, endeavor to obtain for yourselves this blessing ? Will
you not set diligently to work, and ascertain what it is
that you are lacking ?—what it is that hinders you
from possessing this pearl of great price ? If your
tempers are bad, will you not conquer them ? If en-
vious and unjust thoughts rankle in your bosoms,
against neighbor or friend, will you not expell them ?
If sloth or negligence interfere with your own progression or the happiness of others, will you not strive

against and subdue them? If licentious or debasing
pleasures entice you, will you not flee the tempters?
And so, my friends, I might go on to enumerate every
sin or vice that can lead man or woman astray—for all
are enemies to this true love that should reign in your
bosoms, and all must be overcome. One man has to
fight against one enemy, another has something different to contend with, some much more to subdue than
others; but none are so perfect, but that, on rigid
self-examination, they may find a work to do; and
it is one, that no other person can do for them.
Let each one, therefore, set himself or herself to the
task, and banish every feeling and thought from their
minds that is not in harmony with the perfect law of
love—that law which rules the Heavens in their beautiful harmony, and which the angels are so truly and
constantly trying to implant in the hearts of the children of men. Shall we despair because man has so
long fought against its influence? Shall we give up
because no progress is yet perceptible as the effect of
our labors? No, my friends, we shall never weary in
well-doing, and the results of our efforts will now soon
be made more apparent to you. Silently the leaven is
working. One man here, and another there, is beginning to take the right view of things—they are com-
mencing to find out that though it is to revolutionize a
world we come, the work is an individual one, each one
must perform his quota—in his own heart the change
must be; there the revolution must take place, and
when it is thoroughly effected let him try to produce
like effects in others; let him show by his life and
conversation how much he is altered for the better;
let kindness and love, active and untiring, rule his
actions—always ready to prove the truth of his teachings by the benevolence and purity of his conduct; and
the happiness his belief has brought to him, by the

cheerfulness and perfect harmony and love that reigns in his soul and shines forth in his daily life. Such proofs of the truth of his belief, and the good resulting from it, will do more towards convincing mankind of the benefits to be derived from Spiritualism than all the essays or books we may write. One man's daily walk is a better example than fifty lectures, and will carry conviction home to the hearts of more people ; but both are necessary, and therefore we write. We must point out the way, or how can man walk in it, and we have endeavored to do so in the most simple and practical manner.

We have now embraced in our essays most of the subjects necessary to assist a true Spiritual seeker to understand how he must conduct himself if he desire to progress in the true knowledge of these things ; and if he will follow out our teachings faithfully, developing himself in the virtues we have endeavored to describe, and avoiding their opposite vices, he will find he possesses a strength to resist evil, a love of good, a peace and elevation of mind, a kind and sympathizing spirit for all the sufferings of humanity in every form—and more than all, a perfect knowledge and daily experience of this love of God in his soul, that is beyond every other blessing.

J. W.

October 10, 1860.

ON MARRIAGE.

THE subject on which we are going to treat this morning, is one that has been too little considered by the world at large, in its true bearings ; some few enlightened minds have taken it up occasionally, and endeavored to set the matter in a more correct light, but their teachings have not been well received by the mass of mankind ; and even the women, whose cause they advocate, are against them. So it is, with all progressive ideas ; they have to fight their way into existence with much hard contention and opposition, but finally an impression is made. Some few receive the truth into their souls and present it to others— argue it over and over with outsiders—till many, becoming accustomed to hearing the idea so often propounded, give it more consideration, and violent opposition dies out in their minds, to be succeeded by dispassionate examination, and generally a reception of the truth.

This will ultimately be the case in regard to the marriage relation—so misunderstood at this present time, and often the source of so much misery. If men and women rightly comprehended this thing, and acted up to their knowledge, more than half the misery that now obtains in the world, would be done away with. But men and women enter on this sacred tie with no more real thought or consideration about the importance of it, as a general thing, than they would bestow upon the purchase of a horse or a dress. In fact, the fine points of a female are often the man's only consideration, while dress and ornament too frequently engross all the attention of the woman ! With such preparation for spending a life together, what can be anticipated better than the results that inevitably follow? Could they expect any better? Do they deserve any better? I say, as a man sows so he may expect to reap. If he sows the wind, shall he not reap the whirlwind? But we do not come to chide. We blame you not; rather let us show you a more excellent way. Let us first point out the error, and then we shall be more likely to find a way of correcting it.

Men and women were not born to live alone; it is the law of Nature and of God, that they shall find their greatest happiness in the society of each other; but that can only be when congenial minds and dispositions meet. There can be no congeniality between the educated and the ignorant; the profane swearer and the refined spiritualized woman; the old and decrepit with the young and blooming; the avaricious and the liberal-minded; they are in different spheres of thought, and cannot harmonize. A man who marries a wife for her beauty only, will soon tire of that, if it is not united to more lasting qualities of heart and mind. And it is the same with the woman; she must have something more than a fine house or clothes to make her happy; she was not created to be a plaything for man's idle hours, but a helpmate for him; that is, one who is competent to advise, and take sweet counsel with, on any and every trial or event that may rise up in their social or domestic position.

It is too much the habit with men—men of sense, as well as the ignorant—to consider their wives as on a lower plane of development than they are themselves; they take up the idea that women cannot understand such and such things; that they are too deep for them; too abstruse and metaphysical; and that only the ordinary routine of domestic life, and a little light reading, with a touch of the Bible, is necessary for them.

But I see no reason—I know no reason why women should not be as capable of understanding all the wisdom of your Earth, as the men; their faculties are as good, their intuitions generally more correct, and their organizations, being more refined, are more susceptible to the beautiful and true. Why then should they not take their rightful place in your country and in your family? Why should they not have equal rights and privileges with the other sex? If women were more free to act, if they could exert themselves independently, there would not be so many unhappy marriages in your midst; there would be other spheres of action, other resources to employ their minds, or to earn a subsistence. Many and many a poor girl might have been spared a life of misery and degradation, if they had known any choice in this matter; but society is now so constituted, that a girl, who is what you call well brought up, has no other resource than marriage; and even in that, she is not a free agent as the man is; she must wait to be asked, and too often circumstances oblige her to accept one, when her heart is bound up in another. What inharmonies in the domestic circle must result from these things, it is not necessary to point out; you are all well aware of them; many can bear testimony in your own experience; and those who are more fortunately situated, have only to read your daily papers, teeming with accounts of desertions, divorces, and all the attendant results of such a state of things, to be fully convinced of the truth of my assertion.

But is this without remedy? Can no means be adopted to heal these bleeding wounds that rankle in your midst? There are, my friends. The remedy is in your own hands. You can be your own redeemers, if you have only the courage to follow in the way we propose. And in the first place we would say, elevate your women to the place God and Nature designed for them ; let them be your co-laborers in this onward movement ; they are able to take their stand, and work with you ; they are not so weak and feeble, mentally or bodily, as you would like to suppose, having so long looked upon them as toys or drudges. You may not at first judge their ability fairly, but gradually you will come to the true knowledge of it, and find yourselves as well as them, benefited by the change of feeling. Men are constantly preaching and lecturing about the poor Africans and their degraded condition ; let them look nearer home at the situation of their own white women, and first raise them to their proper condition. When this is done and women feel their independence, when they know they can support themselves by any kind of honest industry they may choose to turn to, without sneers and reproach from the men, think you they will barter their persons for a home, however splendid, jewels however rare? No, my friends. The delicate intuitions of the woman will then have play ; she will not become coarse and degraded as you may imagine, but she will acquire an independence of thought and action ; and if she wishes to form the marriage-tie, love in its true meaning ; unity in thought, similarity of tastes, will be the guides to her choice ; and when these are really met with, no laws will be necessary to bind, for there will be no desire to separate. Such should be the foundation of all unions, and unless it is so, it is not a union at all. Man may profess to join the parties in Holy Wedlock, but they are no more joined than if he had never said the words, unless this true union of thoughts and feelings, aspirations and desires, are there.

Understand me, my friends, do not think I wish to do away with the marriage-tie ; as the world is now constituted, something of the kind is necessary ; but I want to put it on a different footing ; it is not right ; it is not just that the man should have all to say in the matter, and the woman be merely a recipient ; she ought to be so placed on your social plane, that she may be perfectly independent in her choice, as much so as the man ; her happiness is as much involved, and even more so, at this present time, because she has fewer resources to turn to ; but when she has taken her true position—the one always intended for her, and which it has taken man so many centuries to see is her right— a change will come over things ; vice in its worst and most repulsive form will be done away with, purer and better influences will prevail ; woman's influence, so long led into wrong channels by her unnatural position, will be used in a new and better way to soften and elevate the man ; to harmonize and spiritualize his rougher nature, and develop in him all the stores of love and wisdom, so bountifully implanted in his soul, but which at present are almost entirely concealed and deadened by the brutalizing effects of circumstances. Hitherto, man's animal passions and his intellectual faculties have had the sway; under the gentle guidance of his true friend, his other self, more wise and ennobling teachings will find entrance ; his whole life and aims will be changed ; happy and blessed in his domestic relations, it will be his earnest endeavor to extend to others the same blessings, that all may rejoice together.

Hasten this time, my friends, by every effort in your power ; every one can do something towards it. If you are uncongenially united, bear your burden patiently, but take care for your children, if you have any, that they do not fall into like error. Educate your sons to respect their sisters, and their female companions. Never allow slighting remarks, such as "*they are only girls ;*" "what do *they* know ?" All these things foster this state of inharmony. Little by little, the evil must be corrected ; and attending to this in your boys, is one great means.

Your girls should also be taught to respect themselves—to look for something higher as the end of their being, than a matrimonial engagement ; give them tastes, pursuits, trades, if necessary, to render them independent of this, at present, ruling principle in the hearts of so many ; let them feel there is something more to live for than dress or show ; that there is a glorious hereafter, for which they must try to fit themselves—cultivate in them a spirit of love and kindness for all ; but especially for those poor unfortunates who need all, and more than they can bestow ; hardened and debased as they too often are, there is in all of them a chord of sympathy that can be reached, if their more favored sisters would go rightly to work to find it ; and to raise and reform these poor misguided ones, is the most needful and blessed work of a truly spiritualized woman. Angels and men will help her in it, and the blessing of God and of the poor redeemed ones will be upon her.

J.

October 12, 1860.

ON SUFFERING.

Suffering, in all its branches, is one of the penalties that man has to endure, as a consequence of mis-applied and perverted natural laws.

If man followed out the teachings of nature and his own unperverted reason, he would soon see the fallacy of many teachings and usages he now adopts as correct ; he would cease from imitation, and no longer follow the multitude to do evil ; the customs and follies of the world, to say nothing of its vices, would no longer usurp a sway over him, but he would seek out for himself the way that should be most conducive to his own happiness, and that of his family and friends, irrespective of others—individualize himself in the true way, and work for the alleviation of all sorrow and misery, wherever it might be found.

Men are apt, when they speak of, or meditate on, suffering, to look only on physical ills, outside and apparent to every casual observer, and these are certainly legion in their number, and require their best efforts to soothe and alleviate. But there are other causes of suffering besides disease or poverty. Mental distresses often produce more acute and depressing misery than even bodily ailments, and are more injurious in their effects on the life-principle—dragging it down into despondency, and frequently terminating their effects in a lunatic asylum or a suicidal death.

Bodily ailments, my friends, are frequently produced by causes at present not quite under your control, although they might be, if people lived, as has been urged in a former essay, in harmony with Nature's laws ; at present, however, they do not do so, and sickness of various kinds is unavoidable. But mental suffering is more under the control of individual efforts. Harmony of thought and feeling is not incompatible with bodily weaknesses, and may be enjoyed by all, if they only pursue the right means to obtain it. Much can be done by the person himself, much by those around him ; but of himself I would first speak ; let him so live in constant watch and control over himself, that no bitter or angry thought shall be allowed entrance—if it comes with its inharmonious suggestions, drive it from you as you would a viper. Never allow yourself to think that others are unkind, ungenerous, uncongenial or untrue, because they may not happen to think and feel as you do ; remember they have minds constituted entirely different to yours—what may interest and benefit you, may take no hold on them ; they think and judge from their own stand-point, and may be quite unable to receive those truths that may be *your highest happiness.* In cases like these, much positive suffering often supervenes, all from the want of a little charity and self-control. Each one should set a guard over himself, each one retain his own opinion—at the same time give his opponent the same privilege and leave him to its enjoyment.

Argument in such cases is always bad, it stirs up contention and discords ; the temper sometimes fails, then more is said than was meant or really believed, and the suffering is intensified to both parties. But where there is a more intimate union than friendship, where the family circle is broken in upon by these miserable wrangles, sometimes on subjects quite immaterial to the parties, as respects their happiness here or hereafter, what an amount of misery is induced! We spirits, who can read the hearts of the children of men, are alone conscious of it. The heavy heart, the sinking spirit, the lost energies and faded person, too frequently attest it ; but men and women are unconscious of the mischief they are doing, and more frequently think they are performing good service for the cause they desire to advocate.

My friends, all contention is wrong, all strife produces suffering—the strong oppress the weak, the rich the poor, and so on. Whenever one tyrannizes over another, there suffering, and of course inharmony, is produced. Let each one follow the perfect law of liberty, and continue therein, giving and receiving the freedom God always destined for his people; it will not lead to licentiousness, or any other vice, if rightly understood; but it is absolutely necessary that it should be enforced and put in practice by all, if they wish to make themselves and others happy. Binding the person in chains is bad enough, but fettering the mind and the feelings is far more to be dreaded. Let all have freedom to follow out their own ideas of happiness. If one is so constituted that society and pleasurable excitements are his delight, let him enjoy them; in such things there is no sin, the sin is in the excess—that he must and will avoid, if he is rightly developed and brought up. If another prefers study and solitude, let him enjoy them; there is no sin only in the excess; each after his own fancy, and each one giving to the other the same privilege he takes himself—the right to be happy his own way.

One must not exalt himself because he thinks he has better teachings, and lives a higher life—the characteristics of the two may be entirely opposite, and what is pleasure to the one may be purgatory to the other. But is that any reason why he should not be as happy in his own way as the more intellectual man in his? Certainly not—he may, indeed, be the happier of the two, if the better feelings of his nature teach him to sympathize with his fellow-creatures, and relieve their sufferings. And after all, my friends, what are you sent into this world for but to develop for a higher? And how must you accomplish this in the best manner? Should not this be your most earnest study—the question for each one to put to himself, and find out for himself? To himself he must stand or fall. If one thinks he has found out the best means of accomplishing this necessary work, let him follow them out earnestly and truly ; but let him not condemn another if he sees a different path up this same mount of progress.

Man does not see the workings of the human mind, but God does, and he will judge accordingly.

Z.

October 14, 1860.

ON ZEAL.

ZEAL, or earnestness in the pursuit of anything, whether of a temporal or spiritual nature; whether relating to science, arts, or the more laborious and daily recurring employments of life, is one of the most desirable and praiseworthy of our moral faculties, if it is guided and governed by discretion; but let it not run wild, my friends; let it not take the reins in its own hands and guide the moral chariot of the soul, or wild will be its erratic course; many its wanderings from the right track; and sometimes, lamentable will be the consequences of its ungoverned proceedings. Let zeal be always accompanied by wisdom and love, and then it is unknown the amount of good it will accomplish; it is the great lever that is to overturn and uproot all prejudices, old customs and old superstitions; everything that has so long militated against the progression and improvement of the human family, in happiness and development of soul; without it, man would never make a move in the right course. Fear of the world, fear of man individually, fear of loss in property or station, would all interfere, and prevent them from giving to their fellow-men, teachings, that their more receptive and mediumistic minds had been capable of receiving. But with zeal to back their knowledge, they become bold as the lion for the cause they advocate, and sway with potent might the minds they wish to convince. Men are persuaded by their words, in a manner that is surprising even to themselves, and they wonder, as did the Apostles of old, from whence came the power that could so move men's minds.

Truth, my friends, will always make more or less headway in the world ; there are always some minds capable of receiving it, but when it is urged upon the attention with the zealous fervor of an earnest believer, how much more progress will it make in the human family. Only be careful, my zealous friends, that you really have the truth, before you commence to run the gauntlet of public opinion, and then you need not fear the result ; it must and will prevail.

My friends, there are many new teachings and new truths, as they call them, being advocated at this time upon your earth. Man has received an access of knowledge very suddenly, and some of it varying very widely from other ; it has created quite a commotion, as I may say, in men's minds—stirring them up to their deepest depths, and bringing to the surface, thoughts and aspirations they knew not where hidden there. All are beginning to look into things for themselves, to a certain extent—even those, who have hitherto left all the serious thinking to be done by their minister or priest. But many are going deeply and earnestly onward in their inquiries, and it behooves those who think they have received the light, and come forward to give it to others, to be very careful that they do not get error mixed up with it ; if they do, their very earnestness in urging their teachings, will be only the more to be deplored. We are now speaking to Spiritualists, more especially, and we make these remarks, which we think are much needed, because we know how many errors have been given through mediums—errors fatal to the cause, if anything could injure it permanently. Such, thanks to a wise and good God, cannot ever be, but the injury falls on the poor receivers of such teachings, and they must be the sufferers if they follow them out. For be assured, my friends, no wise and good spirits could ever wish to teach what would make men worse than they were before spirit communion was established in its present form.

As Spiritualism advances on the earth, and men's minds are more turned to the subject, teachings will be given in more varied forms. Inspirational writings will be frequently the *modus operandi*, and very great good may be done through them, if the medium can keep himself pure from bias, and be willing to give things new and different, to what he has formerly received as truth. And no medium need ever be afraid that spirits who come to benefit and improve the people of Earth, and add to their happiness, will ever give through them, what would have an opposite tendency.

We commenced by speaking of zeal, and we have branched off into the teachings through mediums ; this may seem irrelevant to the subject, but it is not so ; for different mediums influence the minds of the zealous believers and propagators of Spiritualism to an unknown extent. Men are not aware of this, themselves, and think they are giving their own convictions utterance, when it may be only the teachings they have received from some one uninformed spirit, whose mind is not really so far advanced as his own. Every one who goes to mediums, for teachings, should patiently and quietly receive what the spirits may choose to give, without cavil or question ; but after the sitting is over, and the magnetism withdrawn ; let him diligently examine what he has received, in all its bearings ; test it by his own judgment ; weigh it in the balance of his own reason, and if he finds it accord with that—if he finds there the true wisdom that makes for itself a lodgment in his soul, adding to his peaceful and harmonious feelings, making him a better man, a better father, neighbor, friend—those teachings are true and good, and he may give them to the world without fear of consequences.

His zeal may then have full play ; it can do no one injury ; to many, it may do much good service ; for after all, these are the true benefits, spirits come to bring to the earth ; to harmonize the whole human family, to bring all into that love for each other that shall make them, while living here, fit for the life hereafter. Be careful then, my friends, that you give no teachings to the world at large, that do not approve themselves to your own souls ; look into them carefully, and try them faithfully by your own highest standard ; and let none go forth but what will bear the test of this patient investigation ; then, when thoroughly satisfied of their intrinsic worth, utter them boldly, proclaim them on the housetop if need be, and let no fear of man retard your efforts.

Man incurs a fearful responsibility if he gives to the world erroneous teachings ; there are many ready to grasp them ; hungry souls thirsting for knowledge, and unable to distinguish between the true and the false ; and to these they may prove a snare and a curse ; therefore, beware, oh, my friends ! and study diligently in the way I have recommended, and then you need not fear ; but truth and light shall be given you, and your zeal be perfected.

M.

October 15, 1860.